The Happiest Days of Our Lives

The Happiest Days of Our Lives

by Wil Wheaton

MONOLITH PRESS

Pasadena, California
2007

First Printing – June 2007
Jacket designed by Sean Bonner
Cover Copy written by Andrew Hackard

Hardcover:
ISBN 0-9741160-1-7
ISBN-13 978-0-9741160-1-3

Paperback:
ISBN 0-9741160-2-5
ISBN-13 978-0-9741160-2-0

For Ryan and Nolan

Author's Note

Over the last six years, I've written thousands of posts for my blog, talking about every subject imaginable. Nothing generates as much e-mail and as many comments as stories like the ones in this book. It's not surprising, really, because these stories are the most fun to write and are the closest to my heart: stories about being a huge geek, passing my geeky hobbies and values along to my own children, and vividly painting what it meant to grow up in the '70s and come of age in the '80s as part of the video game/D&D/BBS/*Star Wars* figures generation. There are also a couple of stories about an obscure science fiction show I was a part of for a few years, but I don't think anyone really watched that.

Everything in this book originally appeared online in some form or another. Each time, at least one reader told me, "Hey, you should put this into a book some day." I never said it, but that was sort of the idea all along.

I had a wonderful time revisiting the happiest days of my life while I worked on this book. Thanks for letting me share them with you.

Namaste.

Wil Wheaton
June 2007

what a long strange trip it's been

I asked my stepson Ryan what the formula was to find the circumference of a circle if you know its diameter.

"It's C = π × D," he said.

"Thanks," I said. "I can't believe I forgot that."

I grabbed my calculator and entered 3.14 × 186,000,000.

"Why didn't you remember that formula?" he asked.

"Because that part of my brain doesn't get used as frequently as it once did, and even when it got used almost every day, I had a . . . difficult . . . relationship with it."

584,040,000 came up on my display.

"Why did you want to know what it was?" he asked.

"I just had this idea, and I wanted to know something . . ."

I typed in 584,040,000 × 34 and got back 19,857,360,000.

I looked up at him, unable to contain the huge smile that spread across my face.

"I've been riding this planet for almost twenty billion miles," I said.

"Whoa," he said. "That's cool."

"Yeah," I said. "It really is."

the butterfly tree

When I took my daily walk the other evening, I passed a set of twins who live up the block from me. They're girls, in first or second grade. They're painfully adorable little kids who call me "Mr. Wheaton" and always smile and wave when they drive by with their parents. Their names aren't important, but H loves my dogs, Ferris and Riley, and A always wants to know where "the grills" are (as my wife calls them) when Anne and I walk without the dogs.

They were sitting on their driveway, drawing with sidewalk chalk and talking.

"Hi, girls," I said as I passed.

"Hi, Mister Wheaton!" they cooed in adorable unison.

"How are you today?" I asked.

"Good," A said.

H wiped chalk off her fingers and said, "Guess what, Mr. Wheaton! Today? In school? Melissa C. got her name on the board!"

"It's not good to get your name on the board," I said.

"I *never* get my name on the board!" H said.

"I don't ever get *my* name on the board either!" A said.

"That's awesome," I said. "Bye, girls."

"Bye, Mr. Wheaton!"

I took a few steps away, and a long-forgotten first-grade memory of my own rose up and crashed over me in a powerful wave, washing the smile from my face and the joy from my heart. The memory is so clear, I can close my eyes and see everything in detail that astonishes me. It's almost like I cracked open a time capsule that my mind sealed in 1978.

I lived in a rural area of Los Angeles called Sunland. I can only see it through the eyes of a 6-year-old, so the whole place is forever the late '70s, bathed in the golden red sunset of a summer afternoon: tract houses, wide sidewalks, and lots of trees. It was a great place to grow up, but the schools had a really terrible reputation, so my parents put me into a private Christian school that was a few miles from our house.

I really liked school. Learning was fun, and my parents always seemed interested in every new fact or skill I'd picked up each day. I liked going to the chapel to sing songs with everyone, and the playground had swings that went so high, you could jump out of them and fly through the air for a whole minute . . . or five seconds; my memory on that is a little hazy and distorted by time. We didn't have uniforms, but we had to wear corduroy pants and collared polo shirts. I didn't mind, because it was fun to get dressed up for school, and I really liked flipping the collar up and down on the drive there every morning.

I also loved my teacher, Mrs. Gleason. She was about the same age as my parents, had really long blonde hair, always smiled, and wore blue dresses. She was a lot nicer than Mrs. Krocka, a severe woman who was much older, wore her black hair pulled back into a tight bun, and always wore pantsuits. Mrs. Krocka was from Czechoslovakia and spoke with a thick and intimidating accent. As an adult, I wonder now if she was a Soviet Union expatriate, or if maybe her parents fled Europe during or after World War II, but at the time, she was just a mean old lady to me.

Because she taught the second graders, I only had to see Mrs. Krocka once a day, at recess, except for once a month when she taught our music class (which actually wasn't that bad, because we learned how to sing the songs from chapel in Slovak. I didn't understand what I was saying, but it sounded cool . . . sort of like when they had us do the flag pledges.)

I left that school after first grade and forgot both of my teachers until H and A told me about Melissa C. You see, I was a really good kid in first grade. I only got the equivalent of my name on the board once. Unfortunately, it was in front of my entire family. Oh, and everyone else's family, too. It happened during Back to School night. Mrs. Krocka took over for Mrs. Gleason, who was called away at the last minute for some sort of family emergency.

Back to School night was different then from how it was for my kids: back then, parents brought their kids to school and sat at the back of the class while the teacher took the kids through a truncated version of an average school day for a half an hour or so. When the whole thing was over, the kids got to play on the playground while the parents talked with the teachers, signed up for PTA, and did other mysterious adult things.

I was really excited about Back to School night. I put on my green corduroy pants and wore my favorite blue polo with the skinny orange and brown stripes across the top. I let my mom comb my hair and use Suave hairspray to hold it in place.

In 1978, my brother was almost three years old and my sister was about five months old. For whatever reason, my parents couldn't or wouldn't or just didn't get a sitter, so they brought both of my siblings along to Back to School night. I thought it would be cool for them to see me in my class. I *was* the big brother, after all.

We arrived a few minutes early (a rarity with my parents, who would show up an hour late for the end of the world) and I was one of the first kids to slide into my desk, right next to my friend Matthew. I thought he was cool because he had a Bible name.

After the rest of the parents and students filled the room, Mrs. Krocka explained that Mrs. Gleason wouldn't be there, but she'd show the parents what their children did on a usual day.

We started with our pledges to the American and Christian flags, did our daily prayer, and opened our math books. I thought it was really weird that we were doing this stuff at night, and I wondered if the double prayers were such a good idea, but I kept those thoughts to myself. My parents and my little brother were watching, and I wanted to make them all proud of me.

Before we finished the shortened version of the math lesson, I heard my little brother's voice from the back of the room.

"Mommy! I can't see Willow!"

All the parents laughed. Mrs. Krocka spun around from the chalkboard and shot a whithering look toward the back of the room.

I concentrated on my smelly math ditto. It was two columns of four problems, printed in purple ink on paper that dissolved if you erased it too much. I held my oversized pencil tightly in my now-sweating hand and held my breath.

I heard my mom say, softly, "He's right there, Jer Bear."

"Hi Willow!" he called out, louder. "I see you in school!"

The parents all giggled again. To my horror, a giggle escaped from me, too.

Mrs. Krocka looked directly at me. Through colorless, tightly drawn lips, she said, "I do not tolerate outbursts like this in my classroom."

In the front of the class, next to the chalkboard, there was a cork board. Posted on the cork board were the classroom rules and a laminated picture of a tree. Attached to that tree were laminated butterflies, each with a student's name on it. If a student got into any sort of trouble during the day, Mrs. Gleason would take that student's butterfly off the tree and pin it to a different area of the board.

Mrs. Krocka walked to the front of the classroom and was taking my butterfly off the tree before I even realized what was happening. As hard as it had been not to giggle, it now became even more difficult not to cry.

It was so unfair! It wasn't my fault that my stupid parents brought my stupid brother with them! All the adults were laughing, too! Why weren't they in trouble?

Mrs. Krocka returned to Mrs. Gleason's desk and moved on to the next lesson. The remainder of the time in the classroom is lost to my memory, obscured by an overwhelming sense of humiliation and sadness.

When we were done, I met my parents in the hallway outside the class.

"Why did you bring him?!" I said through tears.

I don't remember what they said, but my baby sister started to cry with me. For some reason, this embarrassed me even more than my own crying, and I started to cry harder.

I can only imagine the scene we were making. The next thing I knew, we were walking to my dad's green Volkswagen bus.

I tried to speak through halting sobs on the way. "It . . . wah-huh-huh . . . wasn't my fa-fuh-fuh-fault! Jeremy muh-muh-made me l-l-laugh!"

"I know, Willow," my dad said.

"Wuh-wuh-will you go t-tell her that it wasn't muh-my fault?" I said. "And to puh-put my bu-bu-bu-butter—" I couldn't even get the word out of my mouth. All I could see was my butterfly, with the happy yellow face and pink wings and "Wil" written in black marker, sitting all by itself.

Alone.

Off the tree.

My parents looked at each other. "We have to get home and get Amy into bed," my mom said.

"WHAT?!" I hollered. "That's so un-fuh-fuh-fair!"

I don't remember what they said. I don't remember the drive home. I don't remember what Mrs. Gleason said when she put my butterfly back on the tree the following morning. All I remember is how hurt and angry I was that my parents didn't stand up for me to Mrs. Krocka, who humiliated and embarrassed me in front of my entire class and all

their parents. In fact, while I walked through my
neighborhood and relived this memory, I felt like I
was going to cry all over again.

My parents did the best they could with all of us,
and I don't know why they didn't stand up for me.
Maybe there's more to the story than I remember, or
maybe they were just as intimidated by that hideous
bitch as I was. But it hurt me that they didn't. A lot.

It's always been important to me to stand up for
people who can't stand up for themselves. Honor,
integrity, fairness, and justice are the most
important principles in the entire world to me, and I
never knew exactly why I felt so passionately about
that . . . until now.

I think it started in a butterfly tree, in 1978.

beyond the rim of the starlight

Shortly after we began production on *Next Generation*, people who had been associated with the series for a long time – actors, creative department heads, producers and writers, mostly – asked us if we'd been approached about going to conventions to promote the show.

The rest of the cast didn't know what a *Star Trek* convention was, but I did, because I'd been attending comic book and horror conventions since I was in the sixth grade and my parents gave me permission to go to the Fangioria Weekend of Horrors convention at the Ambassador Hotel.

"Conventions are awesome!" I said at the end of a table read when the subject came up. "There's all these people, and you can watch movies and buy cool stuff, and I bet you they'd let us in for free!"

I was a naïve 14-year-old, and it didn't occur to me that the if the adults in the cast spent one of their days off promoting the show, they would expect compensation that was a bit more substantial than free admission.

If you're unfamiliar with *Star Trek* conventions, this primer from my book *Just A Geek* may be helpful:

> Conventions (or "cons", as they are known among people who are too busy to say "conventions") are part trade show, part collectible show, and part geek-fest. It all adds up to a celebration of everything related to *Star Trek*, and the atmosphere is always festive and excited.
>
> Promoters hire actors, writers, producers and others from the show to give lectures, answer questions, and sign autographs for the fans. There are also people who sell collectibles, bootlegs, and other sci-fi and fantasy oriented merchandise. The organizers usually run episodes of *Star Trek* on a big screen, and there are always costume contests. Oh, the costume contests. Think *Rocky Horror Picture Show*, with less drag, but more singing. In Klingon. Seriously.

The first time I was on stage at a *Star Trek* convention was in Anaheim, right around the time *Next Generation* started. I wasn't there "officially," but my friend and I had gone to check it out, so that if (when) I was asked (told) to attend cons in the future, I'd know what I was getting into. *Star Trek* conventions, he informed me, were very different from the comic book and horror movie conventions I was used to.

The promoter found out I was wandering around the show (after I paid my own admission, of course) and offered me the glorious sum of one hundred bucks – in cash! – to speak for an hour. To a 14-year-old who thought an eight-dollar admission refund was a jackpot, a hundred bucks sounded an awful lot like a million. Without knowing how badly I was being ripped off (the average person who speaks at a convention earns between five and ten thousand dollars for their time, with captains commanding sums in excess of twenty-five thousand), I gleefully accepted the "generous" offer and did my best to answer questions for an hour.

If you think it went well, you haven't spent any quality time recently around a 14-year-old (geek or otherwise) . . . but I got a hundred bucks, which I spent on books and props in the dealer's room. If you read my short story "The Trade," you now know that I learned nothing about negotiation and money management between the ages of eight and fourteen.

When I went to work the following Monday, some of the *Star Trek* veterans who had originally asked us about cons let me know how badly I'd been had. They put me in touch with people who could arrange for me to travel all over the country – to a different city each weekend if I wanted – to promote *Next Generation*, meet fans, and tuck a little money away for college, or maybe even a house one day.

Conventions were different in the late '80s from the way they are now, with one company called Creation using licensing agreements with Viacom and exclusivity agreements with actors to force just about all of the regional promoters out of the market. Back then, there were as many convention promoters as there were Holiday Inns around the country that were willing to host a few hundred Trekkies for a weekend, and every single con had its own unique feeling and fanbase.

I remember going to a convention in Philadelphia with my mom. She got food poisoning. I don't remember a thing about the convention, but I can still see and feel the waiting area in the emergency room: dark wood on the walls, old magazines on the tables and chairs, ugly white and yellow linoleum tiles on the floor. I spent the entire night playing Tetris on my Game Boy and listening to *The Final Cut* on my Walkman, trying not to be too freaked out that my mom was in the hospital and we were a million miles from home. ("A million" was the default value for "a lot" when I was a kid.)

When I was 18 or 19, I learned that even if the microphone really looks like a Magic Wand massager, it's probably not the smartest thing to tell the audience, "Wow! I'm talking into some sort of marital aid!" . . . especially in the middle of the Bible Belt.

I remember flying to New Jersey to do a convention with Marina Sirtis and playing head-to-head Tetris on our Game Boys the entire flight. I had a massive crush on her back then, and though the thought crossed my mind for most of the trip, I didn't have the courage or the nerve to suggest strip head-to-head Tetris when we arrived. In my 16-year-old mind, it totally would have happened if I had just asked.

Once, in Oklahoma, I was a guest at a dinner where I sat with a few other *Trek* actors while some Boy Scouts served us. The menu had barbecued chicken, beef, and bologna.

"Wait," I remember asking the kid, who was about the same age as me, "barbecued bologna?"

"Yeah," he said, "it's center-cut."

Neither one of us knew what that meant, but I'd grown up white-trash enough to know that bologna was not something I wanted to eat, even – no, especially – if it was barbecued. The problem, however, was that barbecued bologna was a local delicacy, and I was seated at the head table. It seemed like every bologna-loving eye in the hall was watching to see what I did.

I ate it, pretended to like it, and until I wrote this paragraph, nobody was the wiser.

At LosCon in Pasadena, right after I'd gotten my driver's license and my first car (a totally bitchin' 1989 Honda Prelude si 4WS, which was one step better than Patrick Stewart's and, therefore, the subject of much backstage teasing) I met my first science fiction idol, Larry Niven.

The meeting went something like this:

23

Me: Oh my god, you're Larry Niven!
Him: Oh my god, you're Wesley on *Star Trek!*
Both: What?
Both: Can I have your autograph?!
Both: Yes!
Both: COOL!

I still have the copies of *Ringworld* and *Ringworld Engineers* that he signed for me.

They weren't all good times, of course. While most of the cons were fantastic, run by guys who really cared about fans and wanted them to have a good time, others were pretty awful, run by complete crooks who wanted to take the fans' money and get out of town before anyone figured out what they were up to. There are a couple of guys who still owe a lot of fans and actors money that we'll never see.

One of those guys (in the pre-Internet days) convinced 15-year-old me that it was a "short drive" from Amarillo to Denton, Texas. Not having the good sense to look on a map for myself, I agreed to do two different cities in two different days. As the drive across Texas entered its third hour without a single recognizable sign of civilization other than Dairy Queen and Stuckey's, I learned an important lesson about not ever trusting anyone.

On countless occasions, a promoter would tell fans one of us was coming to a show, take their money, and then claim that we'd canceled at the last minute. Of course, the only time any of us ever heard about the show was when irate fans wanted to know why we'd backed out of it.

For you damn kids today who have always had e-mail and the Internets and cell phones, it may be hard to picture a world where a Game Boy was high tech, but it's where I came of age. The world seemed bigger then than it does today, and from time to time, I miss driving straight from Paramount to LAX on Friday after work and falling asleep on the red-eye somewhere over New Mexico, still wearing Wesley's helmet hair.

It was a lot of work to travel the country every weekend, and over the years the Holiday Inns all bled together like a smear of Sharpie ink across the heel of my left hand after a marathon autograph session, but there were many more good times than bad. It was fun to see so many different places and people, all united by their love of this thing that I was lucky enough to be part of . . . at least until the *alt.wesley.crusher.die.die.die* thing really got rolling.

There are still a few regional gaming cons and comic cons and Linux cons and cavecons every year, but not many purely *Star Trek* conventions anymore, as far as I can tell. Part of it has to be economics and how hard it is to compete with Creation, but I also blame The Powers That Be for making several years of sucktastic *Trek* that wasn't worth watching, much less traveling to a Holiday Inn to celebrate.

Over the last couple of years, I've begun attending conventions again, but now I go as a fan. I'm glad that I stopped going to cons exclusively for work, because otherwise I don't think I would have ever remembered how much fun they are when you're just there to geek out. Those of us who will cram thirteen of our friends into a hotel room for a weekend to tell awful puns and watch anime have a place to go where we will not only not be laughed at for dressing up but encouraged to do it (except the furries; those weirdos are on their own). We can invade a hotel for a weekend, pretend it's like the cereal convention in *Sandman,* and recover enough hit points to go back and endure our real lives until the next one.

In fact, when the annual Grand Slam convention was held in Pasadena – practically my back yard – in 2006, I only spent one day there as a guest, signing autographs and posing for pictures. It was Sunday, typically a slow day for any convention, and I just didn't feel like sitting at my little table when there was so much cool stuff going on all around me. So I packed up my stuff, trucked it back to my car, grabbed my camera, and did something I haven't done for years: I walked around the Grand Slam convention purely as a fan.

I listened to astronauts talk about doing for real what I used to do for fakes, which was nothing new for me (I've had the great fortune to meet and talk with several different astronauts over the years) but is also something I will never, ever, take for granted. These guys have been telling the same stories for nearly forty years, but whenever they talk about blasting off, or looking back at Earth from orbit, they recreate those moments with such clarity and passion that they could have just stepped out of the capsule after touchdown.

When they were finished, I wandered over to the dealer's room for a bit of shopping and reminiscing.

At one point, I walked past a booth that had lots of classic *Star Wars* toys. My eyes fell on an original model of Darth Vader's TIE Fighter. I had that toy when I was a kid, and just looking at it was like those car commercials where the guy touches the car and gets this rapid-fire burst of images until he takes his hand off of it. I saw myself riding in the car to Kmart with my parents, hoping to buy a new *Star Wars* toy, playing with the toys on the gold shag carpeting in front of the brick fireplace in the house in Sunland, running around the back yard in the fading evening light in the summer of 1980. I piloted my TIE fighter, chasing my brother who piloted a snow speeder. (We weren't afraid to combine Star Wars and He-Man, so why not combine Star Wars and Empire Strikes Back?)

I know I only stood there and looked at it for a few seconds, but it felt like several minutes. I like it when that happens. I restrained myself in ways that were not possible before I had a family to support, and bought only one thing: a little keychain that said "geek" on it. Then, I headed over to the main auditorium to listen to Ron Moore.

I knew Ron was coming to the show because I'd read it in his blog late the night before, and I hoped that I'd get a chance to talk with him one-on-one, but I didn't expect that I'd run right into him backstage before he went on.

He lit up when he saw me. My prepared speech about how I didn't know if he remembered me from 15 years ago flew out of my head. As he closed the distance between us, some of the things he did for my character flashed through my mind: "Yesterday's Enterprise," the first time I got to do something really different on the bridge; "The First Duty," the first (and only) time we saw Wesley interact with his peers, act his age, and witness his angst-ridden humanity; and "Journey's End," the first (and only) time we saw Wesley as an adult, willing to take a principled stand against his father figure, Captain Picard. I felt a surge of emotion well up in my chest. Before I knew the words were coming out of my mouth, I said, "When we worked together on *Next Generation*, I was too young and too immature to appreciate what you gave me as an actor, and what you did for my character. I know it's fifteen years late, but I wanted to thank you."

He smiled warmly. "Thank you," he said. "It really means a lot to me to hear that."

I wanted so badly to tell him how I'd do anything in the world to be on *Battlestar Galactica*, but I couldn't think of a way to say that without spoiling the moment or coming off like a schmuck, so I just congratulated him on his success, and asked him if he had as much creative control as he wanted.

"I do," he said. "I'm very lucky to work with great people, and the network is very supportive of what we want to do. Of course, we battle, but they are always good battles that make the show better."

He was called onto the stage before we could talk any longer, and as he stepped through the curtain to absolutely deafening applause, I felt happy. I've discovered that all I want to do as an artist (whether it's acting, or writing, or whatever) is create something that matters to people. That is true for all the artists I know, particularly the writers. Like Joss Whedon, Ron has done that, and I felt happy for him in a weird I-was-just-talking-to-you way when the crowd went nuts for him.

When Ron was done, I headed out of the convention for some lunch. When I came back into the hall, someone said to me, "Frakes was talking smack about you on stage," and I instantly knew that Jonathan told the "you used to be cool" story.* I laughed out loud and wished there was some way I could stop time long enough to visit with him before I left to pick up my kids.

I found Jonathan backstage and said, "I can tell, just by looking at you . . ."

". . . That you used to be cool," he said. He wrapped his arms around me and hugged me.

"W," he said, "it is so great to see you."

"You too," I said.

"Are you on your way out, or are you hanging around?" he asked.

"I have to go pick up my kids," I said.

---

* This story is in Chapter Seven of *Just A Geek*.

"How are they?"

"They're great. They're teenagers now, you know."

He chuckled and shook his head. "Man, we are getting so old!" I always look for that impish glint I loved when we worked together. It was still in his eye.

"Are you well?" he asked.

"Mostly," I said. "You?"

"I am great, man."

We talked as long as we could, about kids, and houses, and *Star Trek* and work and wives and all the things that I never could have talked about when I was younger. I just adore Jonathan, and I was genuinely sad when I saw that I had to leave to get the kids.

"I gotta go, Jonny," I said, "and I hope that it won't be a year again before I get to see you, but I'm pretty sure it will be."

"You look great, W," he said. Then he pointed at the huge screen that made up the back of the stage, where Avery Brooks talked about his time as Captain Sisko. "But not as good as Avery."

Avery Brooks did look great. He looked cooler than Shaft and more stylish than anyone else in the convention hall.

"He's really fucking up the cool curve for us, isn't he?" I said.

"Ah, don't worry, W," he said with a grin. "I can tell just by looking at you that you used to be cool."

"You too," I said.

Star Trek has changed a lot in twenty years, and so have the conventions, but one thing remains unchanged in two decades: as a speaker and as a fan, taking that Friday red-eye sounds like a pretty cool thing to do.

Wil Wheaton

blue light special

If someone asked you what toy defined your childhood, what would you say? My kids would probably say Game Boy (Ryan) and Micro Machines (Nolan). My brother would probably say NES. My sister would probably say Cabbage Patch Kids. My dad would probably say baseball cards.

My answer comes without a moment's thought or second-guessing: *Star Wars* figures.

They were affordable, easily obtainable at Kmart, and allowed me to create my nine-year-old version of fan fiction, re-enacting scenes from "my most bestest movie ever" or making up my own. My core cast was Han Solo (in Hoth and regular outfits), Luke Skywalker (X-wing fighter or Bespin version), Greedo (shoots second, goddammit, version), Obi-Wan Kenobi (I lost the plastic robe and broke the tip off the light saber version), Princess Leia (pre-slave girl "man I wish I could hit that" version), C-3PO (tarnished version), and R2-D2 (head stopped clicking a long time ago version). They spent a lot of time fighting on Tatooine (torn cardboard backdrop version), flying around while crammed into a TIE fighter (one wing really wants to fall off version), or rolling around the kitchen floor in my LaNdSPEEdR (kEpP YOU hANdS OFF OF It OR ELSE!! version*).

Yeah, I loved my *Star Wars* figures, and I took them everywhere with me. I never owned one of those official carrying cases that looked like C-3PO or anything, but they traveled with me in a Vans shoebox that could double as a Rebel base whenever the need arose.

Last night, Nolan and I ate dinner at Islands. Right after we put our order in, I saw a kid sitting in a booth at the end of our aisle, playing with *Star Wars* figures on his table. It was like looking through a wormhole into 1981, seeing myself in Bob's Big Boy with my parents.

The kid was eight or nine years old, with a mop of shaggy long hair that was probably cut by his mom with the coupon scissors in a chair in the kitchen. He wore a dirty blue Hot Wheels T-shirt, maroon nylon shorts, and Velcro tennis shoes. On the seat next to him, there was an open shoebox. His *Star Wars* figures were lined up on the table in front of him, and he was making two of them fight.

---

* The story of the LaNdSPEEdR is called "The Trade" and can be found in *Just A Geek*.

I fell into the wormhole and landed at the Sunland Kmart in 1981. It was back-to-school season for my brother and me, and we were there to buy clothes and school supplies. My parents never let us feel how poor or white trash we really were back then, so I didn't know that shopping at Kmart and getting an ICEE and a pretzel was a real luxury for us; like all kids, I just took it for granted that we got to have new clothes and treats, because, well, they were there, you know?

After we piled our corduroy pants and collared shirts and Trapper Keepers and economy packs of pencils and wide-ruled paper in our cart, Mom took our three year-old sister with her to the makeup department to get shampoo and whatever moms buy in the makeup department. My brother and I were allowed to go to the toy department.

"Can I spend my allowance?" I asked.

"If that's what you want to do," my mom said, another in a long string of unsuccessful passive/ aggressive attempts to encourage me to save my money for . . . things you save money for, I guess. It was a concept that was entirely alien to me at nine years old.

"Keep an eye on Jeremy," she said, "and don't run in the aisles."

"Okay," I said. As long as Jeremy stood right at my side and didn't bother me while I shopped, and as long as he didn't want to look at anything of his own, it wouldn't be a problem.

I held my brother's hand as we walked carefully, for about three steps, and then started running across the store, past a flashing blue light special, to the toy department. Once there, we dodged past the bicycles and ignored the shelves of board games until we got to the best aisle in the world: the one with the *Star Wars* figures.

Row after row of glorious *Star Wars* figures in blister packs hung from pegs in a wall that stretched up to the sky. Every one of them had a bright orange price tag, cut into a jagged sunburst marked "$1.99!"

The smell of slightly burnt popcorn, kind of like the smell in the Rainbow Theater (where I'd go on countless eighth-grade not-really-but-we-called-them-that-anyway dates and watch *Ghostbusters* over and over again in 1984) hung heavy in the air. I stood there, experiencing what Douglas Coupland would eventually describe as "Optional Paralysis," pondering one of the most difficult and important decisions I would ever make: which *Star Wars* figure would I purchase? They didn't have the Chewbacca that I really wanted – no, *needed* – to fill a gaping hole in my cast of characters. They had lots of droids, but I already had the only two that mattered. They had some cool snow troopers, but they could only fight Han Solo in his Hoth outfit, and I didn't even have a Hoth playset. (It made sense at the time.) They had IG-88, who was kind of cool and had an awesome gun, but it was only in one scene in *The Empire Strikes Back* and didn't even talk. I stood at the wall of toys and wished, as I always did, that I could just get them all and sort them out at home while my jealous friends watched.

My brother said, "Come on, Wil. I want to go look at the Legos."

"In a minute," I said. I flipped through the ones I could reach, hoping that maybe Chewbacca was in the back behind one of the lame figures up front (that's how I found Luke Skywalker in the Bespin outfit, which had a really cool light saber that you could take out of his hand and lose in the back yard the first day you played with it).

"Come *onnnnnnn*, Wil . . ." my brother said, tugging on my hand.

"Quit!" I said. "This is important!"

Lando Calrissian? He was a dick in the movie. There's no way I'm getting him. That guy with the bald head and the light up headphone thing around his head? What is this, the Bespin Cloud City store? I thought.

"Willlllll," my brother whined. Just then, my mom came around the corner.

"Willow, look what I found for you!" She held up a package of Luke Skywalker X-wing pilot Underoos.

"Oh cool!" I said. "Thanks!"

"And I have Batman for you, Jer Bear," she said to my brother.

"Wow! I'm Batman!" he said. "Thanks!"

"Did you find something?" my mom asked, and then pointedly added, "Or are you saving this week?"

"Mom, I want to look at Legos," Jeremy said.

"Okay, Jer, I'll take you," she said.

She started down the aisle and added, "You need to be ready to go when I come back, Wil."

Left alone in the aisle, I could focus and make an informed decision. Suddenly, as if they'd materialized out of thin air, I saw several vehicles and playsets. The playsets were well beyond my budget, squarely in the realm of birthday gifts from relatives. A Death Star playset among them silently mocked me and my LaNdSPEEdR. However, the sunburst stickers on the vehicles were much more reasonable. I did some math in my head. If I saved, I could have my own Millennium Falcon in just a couple of months. If I could convince my mom and dad to let me do extra chores around the house, or if I got a commercial or something, I could even get it sooner!

Wow. The Millennium Falcon. It was so big, it took two hands to fly it. My friend Darryl let me watch as he put his together, and it had *two* sheets of stickers! It had this place where you could hide your figures, and you could recreate that cool chess game and Luke's fight with the training droid thingy!

Could I do it? Could I save my allowance until I had enough to buy it? What if they didn't have it when I was all saved up, though? Then what would I do? Mom would make me put my money in the bank, and I just knew I'd never see it again, while it earned something stupid called "interest."

My brother came running down the aisle, nearly losing his ever-present blue baseball cap in the process.

"Wil! Look! I got an airplane!" He held up one of those balsa wood planes that always broke on the second flight, provided you didn't break them during assembly.

Oh no, I thought, *Mom will be right behind him!* I could hear my sister fussing in the cart as it turned the corner and squeaked up behind me.

"What did you decide, Wil?" my mom said. "Amy's getting fussy and we need to leave."

I hadn't had nearly enough time to make up my mind. This was all a plot by my mom to get me to save my money! I had to stall, so I pretended I didn't hear her.

"Oh, that's uh, neat," I said to my brother. "What's it do?"

It's a plane, you dolt. It flies.

"Wil?" my mom said, a bit of an edge in her voice.

"It's got a propeller, and that means it can fly for a long long long long time!" he said.

"Uh-huh," I said, my eyes darting from the vehicles to the figures to the playsets and back. "That's cool." A stream of numbers and calendar pages flew through my head, accompanied by John Williams' famous theme.

"Wil, I'm going to count to ten, and then we're leaving," my mom said.

Oh no! She was counting! This was serious.

" . . . three . . . four . . . five . . ."

Three? What happened to one and two?

" . . . eight . . . nine . . ." Why couldn't I just make a decision? All the figures sucked. This should be easy.

But there are so many right there, and how can I walk out of the toy department without buying something?! Jeremy has an airplane!

"Ten. What are you doing?"

As if commanded by some unseen puppet master, my hand shot out and grabbed the nearest figure from the rack.

"I'm getting this one," I said. "This one is awesome."

Ha! Take that, mom! Nobody is going to trick me into responsibly saving my money!

"Okay, put it in the cart and let's go."

I looked down at the package in my hands, and saw my triumphant purchase: Lando Calrissian.

In my head, I thought of the worst curse word I could muster the courage to think.

"Wait. Mom!" I said.

"What?"

She stood there, hand on her hip, patience wearing thin. My brother flew his airplane – which, in the package, didn't look anything like an airplane at all – around in little circles. My sister's fussiness was turning to tears. This was my last chance to back out, admit defeat, and tell my mom that I was . . . I was going to save my money.

I took a deep breath, and said, "I, uhm . . ."

My sister scowled and started to cry.

"What?"

The urge to walk out of the store with something in my hand and some stupid sense of victory overwhelmed the more rational thoughts of saving my money for something I really wanted.

"I, uhm, I want to carry it myself," I said.

"Okay, that's fine. Let's just go," she said. I thought of looking back wistfully over my shoulder at the Millennium Falcon, but I was so ashamed of myself, I was certain that I'd be turned into a pillar of carbonite. Instead, I trailed behind my airplane-zooming brother and nap-needing sister while my mother pushed the cart up to the checkout.

"Wil?" said a voice that didn't belong at Kmart in 1981.

I blinked, as the sounds of my infant sister crying were replaced with The Killers and the smell of burnt popcorn was replaced with the smell of a fryer.

"Are you okay?" Nolan asked.

". . . yeah," I said.

"Where did you go just now?" It's a rather mature concept for a 15-year-old, but I vanish into memory so frequently that he knows it when he sees it.

I told him about the kid over his shoulder, with all the *Star Wars* figures lined up on the table. "It's like looking at myself twenty-five years ago," I said, as John Williams' score began a reprise in my head.

He turned around and back. "You had Jar-Jar twenty-five years ago?"

"What?"

I blinked, and looked at the line of figures: Han Solo, Chewbacca, Luke Skywalker, Darth Vader, and way down on the end, there was Jar-Jar Binks.

A needle scratched across the imagined record. In my head, I thought of the worst curse word I could, and directed it at George Lucas.

exactly what I wanted

After dinner, I was hit with a craving for some sort of frozen fruit, so I told Anne that I was going to run to the store and get myself some nice sorbet or something.

"I have a coupon for Cold Stone," she said. "Why don't you take the kids and go there?"

The nearest Cold Stone is in the mall, and it's a bit of an ordeal to get there, park the car, walk across the whole place, deal with the inevitable mob of teenagers, blah blah blah get off my lawn, but when I was a kid and my dad took me for unannounced ice cream, I thought it was the coolest thing in the world.

I walked into the living room and made the offer.

The kids raced to the back of the house in a blur of tennis shoes and falling Wii remotes.

"So that's a 'yes,' I take it?" I said to the empty room.

Several mini-ordeals later, we were at the counter. A teenage girl with a stud in her nose smiled at me and asked if I was ready.

"Yeah," I said. "I'd like the raspberry sorbet." I stopped myself before I could add *the kind that you'd buy in a secondhand store.*

"What size?" she asked.

"Well," I said, "I'd like you to pretend that I'm three years old, and give me an appropriately sized scoop."

Ryan, standing next to me, slowly shook his head. Nolan said nothing, but I saw his shoulders shake a bit as he suppressed a giggle.

She scooped me a tiny little bit of sorbet, and held it up in a cup.

"Is that good? Or would you like more?"

It was a perfectly tiny scoop, exactly what I wanted.

"That's perfect," I said. "Thank you!"

She handed it to me, and I took a bite.

"You'd better slow down there, Turbo," Ryan said.

"Yeah," Nolan added, "you don't want to race through your sorbet too fast."

I put my spoon back into my perfectly tiny scoop of baby-sized sorbet.

"What?"

Ryan burst out laughing.

"Dude," he said, "you drove all the way up here, parked all the way over on the other side of the mall so it'd be easier to find a space . . ."

" . . . walked all the way through the mall," Nolan added.

"All so you could get, like, three bites of ice cream." Ryan said.

"Not ice cream," I said. "Sorbet. Ice cream is too sweet."

Now it was Nolan's turn to laugh. "Oh, I'm sorry. *Sorbet.*"

I looked at the girl behind the counter. She was trying not to giggle, too.

"Yes," I said, "three bites of sorbet, and it's exactly what I wanted." I made a show of taking a tiny bite and dramatically savoring it. "Now are you going to order, or what?"

Someday, when they're parents, they may understand that it's not about the ice cream, or the *sorbet*, or how much of it there is, or where we parked to find a space, as much as it's all about taking my kids out on a Sunday night so we can all have a good-natured laugh at my expense.

It was, in fact, exactly what I wanted.

close your eyes and then it's past

Ryan had a martial arts class in the town where I spent my elementary-school years, and one afternoon when Anne and I took him there it sparked a flood of surprisingly lucid memory flashes:

Racing down the sidewalk, lying down headfirst on my skateboard. Yes, I cracked my chin, and yes, I have the scar.

Getting a drink from the hose. Why does that chemical, vinyl, rubbery water taste so good? And is

47

it really that cold? To this day, I love a drink from the hose when I'm working in the yard, even though it's just as easy to walk into the kitchen and fill up a cup.

✪ ✪ ✪

The barefoot dash across the parking lot, stopping at least once on the white painted lines, before making it into the cool Thrifty drugstore, where ten-cent scoops of double chocolate malted crunch awaited. The cool linoleum and slightly dry-but-cool air-conditioned air inside is as much a part of summer as swimming and staying up late on weeknights. It was especially wonderful if a day in the swimming pool and chlorine-burned eyes put little halos around all the lights inside and made each breath of cool air burn my chest just a little bit.

✪ ✪ ✪

Stargate, Mr. Do!, Super Pac-Man, and Gyruss at Sunland Discount Variety and Hober's Pharmacy (they've blurred together in my memory), grabbing sips of a Slush Puppy between levels. I can still see the Slush Puppy cup sweating on the machine next to my hand while I played.

✪ ✪ ✪

"Wanna go ride bikes? I have cards to put in the spokes!"

"Cool! We'll race up to the whoop-de-dos by the wash!"

I was surprised to realize that in nearly all of my childhood memories, it's hot, it's summer, and it's smoggy.

An older couple lived down the street from me. They had a pomegranate tree in their front yard, and if you asked them nicely you could pick one and take it home with you, where you'd smash it open on the curb and spit the seeds into the street (or at each other). One summer, they ended up with a few hundred boxes of mint chocolate chip ice cream sandwiches, and they gave thirty or so boxes to my parents, who had one of those giant freezers that opened on the top out in the garage. That was the same summer that we got Atari 400 and I got completely hooked on Star Raiders.

I grew up in a tract home in the Northeastern San Fernando Valley. All the homes around us were some variation of stucco with asphalt shingle roofs and dark wooden shutters stuck onto the sides of the street-facing windows. If you've seen *E.T.*, you've seen houses just like the ones I grew up in. Another

1980s film that features a house just like mine is *Poltergeist.* This is the only movie that still scares the everlivingjesusfuck out of me, and every time I hear Kaja Goo Goo's "Too Shy," it reminds me of the afternoon I watched it with my older cousins, stretched out on the floor of our den after swimming in our pool all morning in the middle of summer.

The idea was to watch the very scary movie in the light of day, so that by the time night rolled around, any residual terror would have been washed away by whatever casserole we had for dinner . . . but it didn't quite work out that way. Now, you damn kids today, who grew up with the MTV and the VH-1 and the MTV2 and your baggy pants and your coffee-can exhaust pipes don't remember this, but back in the early '80s, there was this thing called ON TV. It was one of the first cable movie channels (SelecTV and Z Channel are the other two I remember) and predates HBO. Sometimes, between movies, they'd run something called ON Video Jukebox where they'd play these things that were like concert films and often had little stories and cool grass valley switcher video effects.

To ensure that the top-loading, portable (less than 50 pounds and measuring close to 18 inches square and five inches deep) VCR's timer function captured the entire program, my dad would set it to start recording five minutes before the show was set to start and end five minutes after. This resulted in catching ON Video Jukebox pretty regularly, and before *Poltergeist* started, there was this band singing about being shy. I can still see and hear my dad as he stood in the doorway from the den to the pool, silhouetted by the glare of the mid-day sun (thankfully – my dad insisted on wearing a bikini Speedo throughout my entire childhood, regardless of how many of my friends were over to swim), as he said, "They call them 'Kaja Goo Goo' because they sound like they're singing baby talk," before cracking up at his own joke and disappearing into the glare seconds before we heard him splash into the pool.

Poltergeist started up, and I instantly noticed how much the house and neighborhood in the film looked like mine. As the movie went on, I noticed other things that were just like my life: a little sister with a terrifying clown toy, a tree just outside my bedroom window, a swimming pool under construction a few houses over, quasi-hippie parents, and Zelda Rubenstein standing in the middle of my living room hollering about going into the light.

Well, most of that, anyway.

The movie terrified me so much, because it all seemed so plausible and looked so much like my neighborhood, that I put Amy's clown toy in the garage (on top of the freezer with its bounty of ice cream sandwiches, where it was safely out of our house and in the perfect position to scare off any other kids who entertained notions of sneaking one or two out when nobody was looking) before I went to bed, where I slept with the light on in my bedroom. For several nights.

✪ ✪ ✪

Those memories, and a hundred others, flooded over me like a burst dam in the fifteen minutes it took to drive from the freeway to Ryan's class along streets that were at once familiar and alien, as memories twenty-five years distant struggled to reveal themselves through the progress of the last two decades. . . . like the time when I was eight and I didn't have the courage to tell Kelly that it wasn't right to shoot a dove on a telephone wire with his BB gun. I watched in horror as he fired. A little poof of feathers burst out of the dove's side before it flew away.

That haunts me to this day.

my mind is filled with silvery star

You can learn a lot about someone from the songs they listen to, especially if that person is like me and music is much more than just background noise. As an exercise one afternoon, I put my iPod on shuffle and wrote up the immediate – and often most powerful – memory associated with each song. As much as my elementary and middle school years are dominated by sense memories associated with video games and places, my high school memories are inextricably intertwined with pieces of music.

"Cinderella Undercover" by Oingo Boingo – I am driving my brand new 1989 Honda Prelude Si 4WS to work on *Star Trek*. I don't know why, but in all of my memories, it's early morning, it's cold, and it's a little foggy. I loved that car, and I feel compelled to remind you that it was just slightly better than Patrick Stewart's.

"Don't Be Square, Be There" by Adam and the Ants – My friend Guy (who was also my stand-in on TNG) introduced me to Adam and the Ants via the *Kings of the Wild Frontier* album. I can still see the tape, an old TDK number with "Adam and the Ants" on one side and "Kings of the Wild Frontier" on the other, written in Guy's really cool architect writing, in a smoky gray case with no paper insert. Guy lived in Costa Mesa, and after I got my Mac II – in color, with four frakking megabyes of RAM, man! – I'd put it in my car and drive down to Guy's place on the weekend so we could Appletalk our machines together and play NetTrek and Spaceward Ho! People often asked me in interviews how I avoided the drugs and partying scene that claimed the futures . . . and lives . . . of so many of my peers. I've just realized that this is a major reason why: When they were getting high and courting the paparazzi in night clubs they were too young to be in, I was sitting in Guy's house playing really geeky games.

"Still Ill" by The Smiths – When I was in my very early teens, I had one of those massive teenage crushes that consumes your every waking moment and requires you to listen to endless hours of The Smiths in your bedroom wondering why she doesn't like you "in that way." This particular crush was on Kyra, who was so beautiful, and so smart, and so cool, and so a senior when I was a freshman that it was never going to happen. Kyra introduced me to The Smiths (on vinyl, no less) and the Violent Femmes (in her BMW 2002 while we were driving to see *Harvey* at a local college), and was goth before goth was goth. Though I had such a massive crush on her, we were great friends, and she never broke my heart.

"Pale Shelter" by Tears for Fears – I heard this on the radio in my mom's car on my way to my first day at Crescenta Valley High School, and it will always remind me of that day. I was terrified. I remember sitting in first-period history and not even knowing that I was supposed to write "per. 1" on my papers. I remember that it was nothing like I'd seen in movies and on TV, and how the kids in all my classes were so cruel to me. I was shy and I was scared to death, and I was so withdrawn as a result that they all decided I was aloof and arrogant. I never got a chance to correct that first impression. Wow – as I write this, I can feel that terror all over again. I feel it in my muscle memory and in my soul. God, I felt so tiny as I walked across the quad on that first day, like a little kid who lost his mom in the department store. The time I spent at CV was the absolute worst in my life.

"How Beautiful You Are" by The Cure – *Kiss Me, Kiss Me, Kiss Me* was the first compact disc I had, and it's a good thing, too. I love this record so much, I would have worn it out in any other medium. This was also during the "W + K 4EVR" phase, and, nerdy little artist that I was, whenever I heard this song I longed to go with her to Paris and dance in the rain together. You know what I just realized? I don't think I ever told her that I was so fiercely head over heels for her, and she either knew and didn't call me out, or I had the perfect combination of infatuation and insecurity to keep it to myself. I wonder where she is today, and how she's doing?

"Charge of the Batmobile" by Danny Elfman – My best friend, Darin, lived just over one mile from my house, across windy streets up in the hills above La Crescenta. We were such Batman geeks and such stupid teens that we frequently put this song on my tape deck and drove way too fast across those windy streets late at night between our two houses. It's a miracle we never crashed or hurt anyone or anything.

"Phonetic Alphabet – NATO" This is from disc 2 of The Conet Project. I never heard a numbers station in my teens, but I spent a lot of time listening to my shortwave radio and my police scanner (I told you I was a geek) so it reminds me of sitting in the dark (because shortwave listening is so much better when you're in the dark, for some reason), late at night when propagation was better, spinning the dial and thinking it was the coolest thing in the world to hear transmissions from the other side of the planet. I'm glad the Cold War is over, but boy do I miss the shortwave propaganda broadcasts.

And the Conet Project is the perfect coda to this trip in the wayback machine. That invisible woman's voice, sending a message to some unknown person in an unknown land, shot into the ionosphere and back, captured by someone else in another time, is almost too perfect. If I saw it in a movie, I'd never believe it. Good thing this isn't a movie.

"... *romeo, romeo, lima, yankee, november, oscar, oscar, zulu . . . end of message end of t—*"

i am the modren man

My car's fuel light was on, and though it probably had enough gas to get the kids to school and return me back home, I wasn't about to risk calling a tow truck in my bathrobe and slippers somewhere in between, so I used Anne's car to drive the kids to school. When I turned the key to start the engine, her XM radio sprang to life. It was tuned to the '80s station.

Ryan hopped into the car a minute later. Even though I was seriously rocking out to NuShooz, he grabbed the radio and changed it.

"What do you think you're doing?" I said.

"Changing the radio station." Translation: *You are so lame. I rule because I am sixteen.*

"Well, when you're driving in your car, you can change the radio all you want. But when I'm driving,

if you'd like to change the radio, please ask first."
Translation: *I may be lame, but I'm still your parent.*

I backed out of the driveway.

Ryan sighed and rolled his eyes. "May. I. Change.
The. Station." Translation: *You are so lame. Now I
will use the words you requested, but I will deliver
them as sarcastically as possible. I rule because I am
sixteen.*

"No," I said. "You may not." I took a deep breath
and sang, "Baby! Ah-ah-ah-can't wait! Muh-nah-
nah-nah-nah-bop-de-bop Muh-nah-bup-bop-be-
bop!" Translation: *I can be just as annoying to you as
you are to me. Age and treachery will always triumph
over youth and vigor. I rule because I am thirty-three.*

From the back seat, Nolan said, "Wil, this is
really horrible . . . 'radio.' You will note I did not call
it 'music.' " Translation: *I'm not going to join in the
lameness this morning. Rather, I will make a joke to
defuse the tension. I rule because . . . I just do.*

"I know," I said. "But now that I have the power
of horrible '80s pop music, there is nothing that can
stop me."

Ryan and Nolan both said, "What?" Translation:
What?

Before I could dazzle them with another brilliant
non sequitur, the opening strains of "Mr. Roboto"
filled the car.

I stole a sideways glance at Ryan and caught him
stealing a sideways glance at me.

"Is this 'Mr. Roboto'?" he asked. Translation: *Uh-
oh. I love this song, and I know you've heard me*

listening to it in my bedroom. How am I going to maintain my carefully crafted façade of universal indifference?

"Yep," I said. "You're wondering who I am: machine or mannequin! With parts made in Japan, I am the modren man!"

"Did he just say 'modren'?" Nolan said. Translation: *What the hell does modren mean? Can I say "hell" in my thoughts? I guess I can, since nobody can hear me. Hell hell hell. Hell damn hell. Damn damn crap. Crap damn damn hell crap—*

"Indeed he did," I said.

"What is 'modren'?" he said.

"It's Dennis DeYoung's concept-album version of 'modern,' " I said.

"Does this have something to do with mullets?"

"You know it."

"Because the mullet was the official haircut of rock and roll in the '80s," Ryan said. "I remember." Translation: *I was paying attention to you that one time. But you're still lame. Nothing personal.*

I put on my best Dennis DeYoung voice and nudged the volume knob just a bit closer to eleven. "I've got a secret I've been hiding under my skin! My heart is human, my blood is boiling, my brain IBM!"

I glanced at Ryan again. His right leg was bouncing along with the music, and his head was bopping just a little bit. Translation: *Must . . . maintain . . . carefully . . . crafted . . . cool . . . but . . . losing . . . battle . . . against . . . the . . . rock . . .*

I pulled into a long line of cars and waited to make a left.

"Domo arigato, Mr. Roboto, domo . . . domo." I looked in the mirror at Nolan, who was struggling to suppress a smile.

"Domo arigato, Mr. Roboto, domo . . . domo!" I looked at Ryan and pointedly turned up the volume again.

"Domo arigato, Mr. Roboto, domo . . . domo!!" I pulled the middle and ring fingers of my right hand into my palm, and folded my thumb over them. The light changed, and we inched toward the intersection. I subtly rocked the goat back and forth, just at the wrist.

At the top of my lungs, I belted out, *"THANK YOU VERY MUCH-OH, MR. ROBOTO, FOR DOING THE JOBS THAT NOBODY WANTS TO. AND THANK YOU VERY MUCH-OH, MR. ROBOTO, FOR HELPING ME ESCAPE JUST WHEN I NEEDED TO!"* Ryan shook his head and began to smile.

"Thank you! Thank you, thank you! I want to thank you, please, thank you!" I sang, a bit of Shatner creeping into my Dennis DeYoung.

Ryan laughed. Translation: *Okay, you're still lame, and I'm still so cool because I'm sixteen, but we've got a long history together, and now that I realize you're not buying into my bullshit – yeah, I said bullshit. What are you going to do about it? – I'm going to give it up and enjoy this. Because I am sixteen, not only do I rule, but I can completely change my attitude in a nanosecond.*

Traffic grew heavier as we got closer to the school. I turned the radio down to a reasonable volume. Translation: *I don't need to embarrass you in front of your peers . . . this time.*

"The time has come at last to throw away this mask, so everyone can see my true identity . . ." I sang.

Ryan joined me: "I'm Kilroy! Kilroy! Kilroy! Kilroy!" Translation: *See? I may be totally cool because I'm sixteen, but I'm not totally lame, either. Remember, you must learn how to deal with me now, because my brain is all messed up. I'm not trying to be a jerk. Honest. I can't help it sometimes.*

"Who is Kilroy?" Nolan said.

"I have no idea," I said, as I pulled to the curb and they opened the doors. "But you can be sure he wore a mullet."

They nodded at me and smiled. Sort of. Translation: *Just nod, smile, and walk away.*

"I love you guys," I said. "Have a great day." Translation: *I love you guys. Have a great day.*

"Okay," they said, "we will." Translation: *We love you, too. Even though you're totally lame.*

I pulled away from the curb as Mötley Crüe's "Home Sweet Home" began to play.

I sang, "You know I'm a dreamer, but my heart's of gold . . ." No translation necessary.

suddenly it's tomorrow

Thousands of people swarmed around the Rose Bowl, about 1,500 of them ahead of us in the runners' starting corral and another 5,000 or 6,000 in the walkers' area beside us. The sun felt warm on my face, and I wondered if I'd made a mistake wearing my long-sleeved shirt.

I stood with my entire family as we prepared to run in the annual Susan G. Komen Foundation's 5K Race for the Cure. Originally, it was just going to be Nolan and me, but Anne got interested, and then Ryan decided to round it out to a full-on family event. Anne's friend Michelle joined, too, and so did our friend Amanda. Suddenly, without really trying, we were a team.

"Do I have to stay with you if you're going too slow?" Nolan asked me.

I told him that he didn't, and we all agreed to meet under the giant American Airlines balloon that was set up on the South Lawn when we were all finished. We stretched, did some ridiculous-looking jumping around to get the blood pumping, and waited for the race to start.

The gun went off, and the kids broke away from us after about six strides.

"Wow! Look at them go!" Amanda said.

"Yeah, I suspect we'll be catching up with them around the second mile," I said, as we passed a troupe of Japanese Taiko drummers. For reasons that I'll never fully understand, Taiko has always inspired me at a cellular level. It's like those rhythms get into my nanosoul, and I started out a little fast as a result. After about a quarter-mile, my Garmin Forerunner was chirping at me that I needed to slow down, and I'd pulled far away from Amanda, Anne, and Michelle. Still no sign of Nolan and Ryan, though.

I felt pretty good, considering that I hadn't put my shoes on in over five weeks, no thanks to an incredibly annoying groin injury that showed up suddenly in December and sidelined me until the day before the race. I cruised along for the first mile, smiling at people, announcing "On your left!" and "Looking great!" to the little kids who were running with their parents. I felt good, emotionally and physically. I loved it that I was out here on a Sunday morning with thousands of people, and I loved it that I was in my first race of 2005.

I sent some mental probes along my body, to see how I was doing:

- *Feet:* Feeling great!
- *Legs:* A little tight, but warming up nicely.
- *Back and shoulders:* Five by five, captain.
- *Cardiovascular system:* If you don't get faster than 9 minutes a mile, we'll be just fine, sir.
- *Right groin and hip area:* Houston, we have a problem.

Oh, shit.

Truth be told, I shouldn't have run, and I put myself right out of the San Diego marathon later that year by running through the pain, but I *desperately* ~~wanted~~ needed to spend some time with my family. For months, I'd spent more time down at ACME working on sketch comedy shows than I spent at home. When I was home, I spent my time working so hard to meet my writing commitments, I hardly had any time to just sit and visit with Anne and the kids. I was constantly distracted by all my commitments and had to fight the urge to rewrite things in my head when I wasn't sitting in my office, during time I'd planned to set aside for my family. I'd been redlining for weeks, and I was exhausted, creatively and otherwise. I vowed that, whenever I got a free moment, I would spend it with my family, but my free moments were few and far between.

So.

Just short of mile one, I felt the first twinge of pain in my right hip. "Look," I told my body, "we're just doing 5K, and our pace is 10 minutes per mile, so relax, okay?"

"Yeah, probably not," my body said. Pain began to radiate around my hip and up my chest. Right around 1.3 miles, I had to slow down, and at 1.5 miles the pain was so intense I had to walk.

Goddammit! For the first time since it happened two years before, I really felt like I was in my thirties. I mean, in my bones, in my heart, and especially in my muscles.

A cheerful voice behind me called out, "On your right!" A woman in her 60s wearing a pink "I'm a survivor" T-shirt jogged past me, putting everything into perspective.

"Doing great!" I said when she was ahead of me. She didn't look back, but flashed an enthusiastic thumbs-up.

I walked quickly for a few minutes. When the pain began to subside, I tried jogging lightly. I went slowly but steadily, and caught up to Ryan near mile two.

"Hey! How are you feeling?" I said.

"My knees are killing me," he said, "and Nolan ran faster than I've ever seen him run. He was all the way up in the front, where there were only ten or fifteen people, when I had to walk."

"Well, you want to run with me?" I said.

"I don't think so," he said. "I'll see you at the finish."

No way, kiddo. This is why I came out here today, I thought.

I slowed and walked with him.

"What are you doing?" he asked.

"I'm walking with you!" I said.

"Oh. Cool," he said. He was *so* fifteen that I couldn't tell if "cool" meant "cool" or "you're so lame, Wil," but I was happy to walk with him.

We moved slowly through a few other walkers. A man jogged past us, pushing his 3- or 4-year-old daughter in a jogging stroller.

"We're doing great, daddy!" she said with a huge smile.

"We . . . sure . . . are . . . honey," he said. He was not smiling.

Right around mile 1.9, Amanda caught up to us.

"Hey, I know you!" Ryan said.

"How are you guys doing?" she asked. She was training for the L.A. Marathon, so this was nothing to her.

"My stupid hip is giving me a really bad time, but other than that I'm fine," I said.

Ryan told her about his knees, and we did a little speed-walking for a few minutes, until I saw the water station for mile two at the crest of a little hill.

"I'm going to run the last mile," I said. "I'll either see you guys at the finish or you'll step over my body in about 3,000 feet."

They wished me well, and I began to jog. I extended my arm – just like a real runner – as I passed through the water station. A smiling middle-schooler pushed a Dixie cup into my hand and said, "Great job!"

"Thank you!" I said as I dumped the water over my face and head. I was on the western side of the Rose Bowl now, heading south. The sun was in my face, and I began to regret wearing my long-sleeved shirt.

The Rose Bowl has been involved in several landmark moments in my life, most of them when I was a teenager living in La Crescenta: When I was fourteen, I attended the Depeche Mode Concert for the Masses there. When I was fifteen, my best friend Darin taught me how to drive a stick shift in his VW Bug . . . right in the parking lot that was now on my left. My hip was on fire, and I was beginning to feel dangerously warm in my long sleeves, but I smiled. *This is a great way to spend a Sunday morning,* I thought.

When I rounded the penultimate corner in the race, I was breathing hard. The sun was beating down on me through a magnifying glass, in classic Warner Brothers cartoon-style, and I pushed my sleeves up as far as they could go. I sprayed the remainder of my water over my face and immediately felt better. I turned north and checked my Forerunner: I had less than a quarter of a mile to go. Surprisingly, the pain in my hip, groin, and ribs wasn't that bad. Maybe it had just been masked by adrenaline so I could finish, but I've learned that there are times when you just don't ask questions. I was in the final 1,000 meters! Music and cheering filled the air.

I set my eyes on the finish line, and the noise of the crowd faded away. Pretty soon, all I could hear was my heartbeat in my ears and the pounding of my feet on the pavement. With about thirty yards to go, I heard a familiar voice calling out, "Go Wil! You're almost there! Go! Go! Go!"

I blinked my eyes and looked off to my right. There was Nolan, grinning broadly and jumping up and down. It was pure, concentrated mojo. I raised one of my hands up and made it into a fist. I pumped it in the air at him.

"Yeah! Go Wil! Go Wil!" he cheered. My heart swelled, and I finished the race running on air.

I crossed the finish line and got my time: 34 minutes. Not bad, all things considered. My body ached, my throat was dry, and my heart pounded fiercely in my chest. My 3.1 miles felt more like a marathon, which was a sad commentary on my current level of physical fitness, but I did it! I ran slower than my marathon training pace, but I did it! I ~~wanted~~ needed to spend some time building memories with my family, and *I did it!*

When I got off the course, I collapsed into the grass and caught my breath. After a few minutes, I stretched. The pain in my hip was slowly coming back, but Nolan's cheering echoed in my head, and there wasn't any pain at all strong enough to break through *that* wall of joy.

Eventually, I made my way over to our meeting place. Ten minutes or so later, Ryan and Amanda came over.

"What was your time?" I asked them.

"Thirty-six," Ryan said. "What was yours?"

"Thirty-four."

"Nice job," he said. I ran this comment through my fifteen-year-old-to-English filter and got "*Nice job [Sincere.]*"

"Thank you, Ryan," I said with a grin.

Behind us, on the other side of the giant American Airlines balloon, about fifty people were Jazzercising. Outrageously loud Europop music assaulted our weary ears, but the Jazzercisers seemed to enjoy it.

I always thought Jazzercise was an improv joke, you know, like "Biggus Dickus." But it turns out it's a real thing, and the people doing it were having a *really* good time. When the music went out (presumably because the girl leading them whooped and blew out the mixer), they kept right on going while she said things like, "Up to the left! Up to the left! And attitude! And attitude! Left! Left! Give me attitude! Attitude!"

Anne, Michelle, and Nolan walked up together.

"I learned something today," I said.

"What's that?" Anne said.

"Jazzercising is all about attitude," I said.

She sat down next to me.

"How'd you do?" I asked her.

"I totally ran the whole way!" she said. She was the happiest I'd seen her in weeks. She had also been under a lot of stress and pressure, so seeing her smile and relax nearly brought tears to my eyes.

"I'm really proud of you, honey," I said.

We talked about our times, and I turned to Nolan.

"I loved it that you were cheering for me, Nolan," I said. "Thank you."

"Of course," he said. He was thirteen, and the inevitable day when I'd have to start using the English translator hadn't yet arrived.

"What was your time?" I asked.

"Twenty-four minutes!" he said.

"Holy crap, Nolan!" I said. "That's fast!"

"Yeah, it was fun," he said. "I think I finished pretty close to the top."

"Gosh, you think?" I said.

The Jazzercise music started up again.

"What the—" Anne said.

"Attitude," I said, "plus loud Europop, equals Jazzercise."

We snacked for a few more minutes, picked up our stuff from the gear-check, and headed back to our car. As we crossed the street, thousands of walkers streamed across the bridge and turned into the final stretch. They were a sea of pink shirts, pink hats, pink balloons, pink flags. They were singing and shouting and having a great time.

"Oh my god," Anne said, "look at all those people!"

We did.

"We are totally part of that," I said. "I'm proud of us. All of us."

a portrait of the artist as a young geek

December, 1983

I sat on the floor in Aunt Val's house and opened up her Christmas present to me. It was a red box with a really cool-looking dragon on the front of it. Inside, there were a few books, some dice, a map, and a crayon to color in the dice.

"That's a game that I hear lots of kids like to play, Willow," she said. "It's dragons and wizards and those things you liked from *The Hobbit*. The back says you use your imagination, and I know what a great imagination you have." My brother played with Legos and my cousins played with handheld electronic games. I felt a little gypped.

"Wow," I said, masking my disappointment. "Thanks, Aunt Val!"

Later, while the other kids played with Simon and Mattel Electronic Football, I sat near the fireplace and examined my gift. It said that I could be a wizard or a fighter, but there weren't any pieces that looked like that. There were a lot of weird dice, but I had to color in the numbers. That seemed silly, but at least it was something to do, so I grabbed the black crayon and rubbed it over the pale blue dice, just like the instructions said.

Aunt Val (who was my favorite relative in the world throughout my entire childhood and right up until she died a few years ago) walked into the living room. "What do you think, Willow?"

"I colored the dice," I said, and showed her the result. "But I haven't read the book yet."

She patted my leg. "Well, I hope you like it." She moved to the other side of the room, where my cousin Jack poked at a Nintendo Game and Watch.

I opened the *Player's Guide* and began to read.

February, 1984

It was afternoon PE in fifth grade, and I was terrified. I ran and jumped and ducked, surrounded by a jeering crowd of my classmates. The PE teacher did nothing to stop the attack – and, in fact, encouraged it.

"Get him!" someone yelled as I fell to the asphalt, small rocks digging into my palms. I breathed hard.

Through my adrenaline-fueled flight-or-fight response, the world slowed, the jeering faded, and I wondered to myself why our playground was just a parking lot and why we had to wear corduroy pants in the middle of a Southern California heat wave. Before I could offer any answers, a clear and loud voice spoke from within my head. "Hey," it said. "You'd better get up and move, or you're dead."

I nodded my head and looked up in time to see the red playground ball, spinning in slow motion, as the word "Voit" rotated into view. Pain exploded across my face and a mighty cheer erupted from the crowd. The PE teacher blew her whistle.

I don't know how I managed to be the last kid standing on our team. I usually ran right to the front of the court so I could get knocked out quickly and (hopefully) painlessly before the good players got worked up by the furor of battle and started taking head shots, but I'd been stricken by a bout of temporary insanity – possibly caused by the heat – on this February day, and I'd actually played to win the game, using a very simple strategy: run like hell and hope to get lucky.

I blinked back tears as I looked up at Jimmie Just, who had delivered the fatal blow. Jimmie was the playground bully. He spent as much time in the principal's office as he did in our classroom, and he was the most feared dodgeball player at the Lutheran School of the Foothills.

He laughed at me, his long hair stuck to his face in sweaty mats, and sneered. "Nice try, Wil the Pill."

I picked myself up off the ground, determined not to cry. I sucked in deep breaths of air through my nose.

Mrs. Cooper, the PE teacher, walked over to me. "Are you okay, Wil?" she asked.

"Uh-huh," I lied. Anything more than that and I risked breaking down into humiliating sobs that would follow me around the rest of the school year, and probably on into sixth grade.

"Why don't you go wash off your face," she said, not unkindly, "and sit down for a minute."

"Okay," I said. I walked slowly across the blacktop to the drinking fountains. Maybe if I really took my time, I could run out the clock and I wouldn't have to play another stupid dodgeball game.

January, 1984

Papers scattered across my bed appeared to be homework to the casual observer, but to me they were people. A thief, a couple of wizards, some fighters: a party of adventurers who desperately wanted to storm The Keep on the Borderlands. But without anyone to guide them, they sat alone, trapped in the purgatory of my bedroom, straining behind college-ruled blue lines to come to life.

I tried to recruit my younger brother to play with me, but he was 7, and more interested in Monchichi. The kids in my neighborhood were more interested in football and riding bikes, so I was left to read through module B2 by myself, wandering the Caves of Chaos and dodging Lizard Men alone.

February, 1984

I washed my face and drank deeply from the drinking fountain. By the time I made it back to the benches along the playground's southern edge, I'd lost the urge to cry, but my face radiated enough heat to compete with the blistering La Crescenta sun.

I sat down near Simon Teele, who, thanks to the wonders of alphabetization, ended up with me and Harry Yan (the school's lone Asian kid) on field trips, on fire drills, and in chapel. Simon was taller than all of us, wore his hair down into his face, and really kept to himself. He was reading an oversized book that sort of looked like a textbook, filled with charts and tables.

We weren't officially friends, but I knew him well enough to make polite conversation.

"Hey," I said. "Why don't you have to play dodgeball?"

"Asthma," he said.

"Lucky," I said. "I hate dodgeball."

"Everyone hates dodgeball," he said, "except Jimmie Just."

"Yeah," I said, relieved to hear someone else say out loud what I'd been thinking since fourth grade.

"Hey," I said. "What are you reading?"

He held up the book and I saw its cover: a giant statue, illuminated by torches, sat behind an archway. Two guys were on its head, prying loose one of its jeweled eyes, as a group of people stood at the base. One was clearly a wizard; another was obviously a knight.

"Player's Handbook," he said. "Do you play D&D?"

I gasped. According to our ultra-religious school, D&D was Satanic. I looked up for teachers, but none were nearby. A hundred feet away on the playground, another game of dodgeball was underway. I involuntarily flinched when I heard the hollow *pang!* of the ball as it skipped off the ground.

"You're going to get in trouble if you get caught with that," I said.

"No, I won't," he said. "If I just keep it turned upside down, they'll never see it. So do you play or not?"

"I have the red box set," I said, "and a bunch of characters, but I don't have anyone to play with."

"That's Basic," he said. "This is Advanced."

"Oh."

"But if you want, you could come over to my house this weekend and we could play."

I couldn't believe my good luck. With a dodgeball to the face, Fate put me on the bench next to the kid who, over the next few months, helped me take my first tentative steps down the path to geekdom. He had a ton of AD&D books: the *Dungeon Master's Guide*, which had a truly terrifying demon on the cover, and would result in certain expulsion if seen at school; the *Monster Manual*, which was filled with dragons; and the *Fiend Folio*, which not only had demons and devils, but a harpy and a nymph, accompanied by a drawing of a naked woman! with *boobs!!*

Simon's parents were divorced, and he lived with his mom in a huge house in La Canada. His room was filled with evidence of a custody Cold War. Too many toys to count littered the floor and spilled out of the closet, but even though we were surrounded by Atari and Intellivision, GI Joe and Transformers, we had D&D fever, and the only prescription was more polyhedral dice.

Though it was just the two of us playing, we stormed the Keep on the Borderlands and explored the Isle of Dread. We spent all our free time at school making new characters, designing dungeons, and unsuccessfully attempting to recruit other kids to play with us.

March, 1984

My babysitter Gina's older brother was an experienced Dungeon Master, and he let us play in one of his custom-made dungeons. My fighter walked into a room, got trapped behind a portcullis, and died when I sprang a trap trying to escape. Simon and I decided later that it would be okay to resurrect him for our own adventures without penalty, because Gina's brother's dungeon was really too hard, and it wasn't part of our world, anyway.

June, 1984

Simon and I finally got two other kids to join our group: Robert and his friend David. The four of us were officially declared "the nerds" by the cool kids at school, and we played almost every weekend. I started carrying my dice, a couple of pencils, and folded-up character sheets with me everywhere I went, stored in a pleather Casio calculator case that my dad gave me.

The Satanic Panic, fueled by Jack Chick's "Dark Dungeons" and some "investigative" reporting on television news magazines, reached our suburban school. I brought home a letter from school warning our parents about the dangers of *Dungeons and Dragons*. My parents laughed it off, but Robert's did not; he was prohibited from playing with us any more, and since he brought David into our little group, David left too. Then, right when school was about to get out for summer, we were dealt a total party kill: Simon's mom was moving the two of them to Indiana.

July, 1984

With Simon gone and the Satanic Panic at its peak, I didn't have anyone to play with. My books and character sheets slowly made their way into my closet as Atari began to creep further and further into my life. Then, for my birthday, Aunt Val gave me a book called *Lone Wolf*. It was like Choose Your Own Adventure, but you had a character sheet and rolled dice for combat! It wasn't D&D, but it was close enough.

1987

I was a freshman in high school and gained admittance to a group of geeks via my friend Darin. We played tons of geeky games together, watched *Holy Grail* at least once a month, and argued the finer points of sci-fi. I was finally surrounded by geeks again, only this time I was proud to be counted among their number.

One day, sitting in Darin's house and playing *Illuminati*, I said, "Hey, do any of you guys ever play D&D?"

There was a collective snort of derision.

"What?" I said.

"We play *GURPS*," one of them said.

"What's that?" I said.

A knowing look passed among them. Within a few weeks, I started in my first Space/Old West/Magic campaign.

June, 1992: The Dark Ages

I met and began dating a girl who didn't appreciate gaming at all and thought it was entirely for nerds. I collected my games and put them all into storage.

March, 1993: The Renaissance

We broke up. The games came back out of storage. I'm pretty sure my 40K Space Marine armies held a bit of a grudge.

1999

After living together for three years, my girlfriend and I moved out of Sin and into Married Life. I began counting the days until I could introduce her children, who I was raising as if they were my own, to the wonderful world of gaming.

After we'd spent about six years in each other's lives, I began gradually to introduce the kids to some of the geekier things I like. By the time the *Lord of the Rings* movies came out, they were ready to take their first steps down a path that began in a tavern and ended in a dragon's lair.

February, 2004

The boys and I spent a week or so creating characters and discussing the rules, building excitement for the adventure. I stayed up way too late each night after the kids went to bed, poring over websites and my rule books, simulating combats and creating NPCs. It was the first time I'd run an adventure since *The Isle of Dread* in sixth grade, when I scored a Total Party Kill during the first encounter. I never got to sit behind the screen again.

I sat at the dining room table and reviewed cleric spells while the *Two Towers* soundtrack inspired my imagination. Ryan came out of his room and sat down across from me.

"Whatcha doing?" he asked.

"Just refreshing my memory. It's been—" I paused. "Well, it's been a really long time since I ran a campaign, and I want . . ."

I want you to think I'm cool. I want to do something special for you. I want to share something with you that isn't sports-related, so your dad can't take it over and force me out of it.

"I want to make sure you guys have a good time," I said. "It's important to me."

"I'm so excited!" he said.

"Me too."

He absentmindedly rolled some d20s I'd scattered across the table.

"Can I roll up an extra character, just for fun?" he said.

"Is your homework finished?"

"Yeah. Everything's done, and I worked ahead in Biology."

"Really?"

He nodded.

"Dude. That's super-responsible. I'm proud of you."

He smiled. "So can I?"

"Sure," I said. "The dice bags are on my desk."

He walked over to my office. My desk, normally buried under computer books and writing journals, was covered with gaming books: *GURPS*, *Mutants and Masterminds*, *Car Wars*, too many Cheapass games to count, and – of course – a stack of D&D books ten feet tall.

"It's 4d6, right?" he called out.

"Yep, 4d6. And you—"

"—throw away the lowest roll," we said in unison.

"Ryan, I . . ."

I love it when that happens.

"I have an extra character sheet here that you can use."

"Okay."

I went back to my books. A moment later, four six-sided dice dropped from Ryan's hand and rolled across the table.

"Since you're the DM, will you watch my rolls?"

"You bet! This is . . ."

This is something I'll remember for the rest of my life.

"This is really fun."

He picked up the dice and threw them: 2 – 4 – 5 – 1.

"Eleven?! Oh man!" he said.

"Eleven isn't a bad roll at all." I noticed something familiar about the dice. Two of them were black, with red numbers. There was a skull where the 1 would have been.

"Hey, I have dice just like those in—"

My heart stopped. I ran into my office.

There it was, in the cool blue glow of my monitor, atop my *Freedom City* sourcebook: an open bag of dice. *My* bag of dice. The black one, with the red pyramid from the Bavarian Illuminati on it. A clear d10 and two brilliant blue d12s sat near its open top. Its drawstring was cast carelessly across the side of the book, dangerously close to my Zen fountain.

Ryan slowly walked into the room.

"Is something wrong?" he asked.

"You . . . you touched my dice!" I felt a little woozy.

"Well . . . yeah."

"No, Ryan, you . . ."

You are about to see your stepdad as the old gamer geek he really is. The gamer geek I hope you'll be one day . . . you know, this is actually kind of cool.

"You can't ever touch my dice," I said, patiently.

"Uhh . . . aren't they all," he made quote marks with his fingers, " 'your dice'?"

"Technically, yes, but these here, in this bag, they're the ones I've played with since I was in high school."

He furrowed his brow and looked at me while I put "my dice" back into my bag. A white d8 with worn-off blue numbers, the clear d10 with white numbers, a green d6 that's really a poker die . . .

"When I was younger, these dice . . ."

These dice were some of the most important things in my life. Well, I have some perspective now.

"These dice were a big part of my life," I said.

I held the bag in my hand and looked at him. For the first time in eight years, I saw some of myself reflected back.

"You know what? It's not that big a deal. I'd just rather you used some other dice," I said.

"So can I re-roll that eleven since I used . . ." He lowered his head, and spoke in a grave voice: "The Forbidden Dice?"

We laughed together.

"Eleven is a good roll, Ryan."

"I know, but twelve gets me plus one."

"Okay. You can re-roll. But if you get a lower roll, you have to keep it."

I tossed him my green "community" bag.

"Deal," he said, as he dug out four dice.

We walked back into the dining room and sat back down at the table. Ryan threw 2 – 5 – 2 – 1.

"Nine?! Oh man!"

"I bet that eleven is looking pretty good now, isn't it?"

"Shut up." He laughed.

He collected the dice, held them thoughtfully for a second, and said, "Wil, I'm sorry I used your dice. I just thought that bag was really cool."

"It's okay, Ryan. Someday . . ."

Someday, I'll give that bag, and all the dice in it, to you.

"Someday, you'll have your own dice, and your own dice bag, and you'll understand."

He threw 4d6: 6 – 6 – 4 – 4.

"Sixteen! Rock!" He threw the goat.

On an index card, he wrote a one and a six beneath his nine.

"Ryan, I . . ."

I love you more than you'll ever know. Thank you for sharing these moments with me.

"I can't wait to play with you guys tomorrow night."

June, 2007

As much as I want to, I can't hate dodgeball or the "cool" kids who tormented me throughout the years. Without that influence, I probably wouldn't have discovered gaming, and no single thing contributes as much to my geekiness or brings me as much joy.

I still flinch when I hear that hollow *pang!* of a dodgeball, though. That's a saving throw I think I'll always fail.

the big goodbye

L ast week, I went to Paramount to film some host wraps for a *Star Trek: TNG* DVD documentary, and I discovered that the old cliché is true: you can't go home again, especially when your home has been torn down and replaced with sets for a Farrelly Brothers movie.

It wasn't the first time I'd been to Paramount since Wesley Crusher turned into a magic ball of light and floated out into the galaxy to fight crime and save amusement parks from evil developers with The Traveler. In *Just A Geek*, I wrote:

> I found myself at the Melrose Avenue guard shack, half an hour early for my 8:30 a.m. call time.
> "ID, please," the guard said.
> I pulled my driver's license out of my wallet and gave it to him.

"And where are you going today . . ." he looked at my license, "Wil?"

"I'm working on *Star Trek*," I said.

"*Enterprise* or *Nemesis*?"

The Next Generation, I thought.

"*Nemesis*," I said. "I play Wesley Crusher."

He looked up at me. "Oh my god. You *are* Wesley Crusher! You look so . . ."

Washed up?

". . . grown up."

"Yeah," I said, "it's been a long time."

"Do you know where to park?"

"Yeah. But I don't know where our dressing rooms are."

But I do! I do know where our dressing rooms are! They're trailers on the street in front of stages 8 and 9. Mine is filled with Warhammer 40K *figures and* GURPS *books. It's right next to Brent's trailer. It's 1989, and I'm back. I'm back home.*

When I worked on *Nemesis* several years ago, returning to Paramount to put on the uniform and immerse myself – if only for a day – in Wesley Crusher's goofy grin and wide-eyed excitement (I wrote at the time that I couldn't tell where Wesley ended and I began), it was an emotional experience. I felt genuine regret for not appreciating *Star Trek* more when I was on the series every day, which morphed into a general regret that when I was a teenager, I acted like . . . a teenager. Some of *Just A Geek* is about this, and the catharsis that came from writing it is a large reason why I was able to accept and embrace my small role in the *Star Trek* universe.

I went to Paramount last week to go onto our old stages and walk a camera crew through the Guardian of Forever into 1987. I didn't expect to be particularly emotional. I was wrong.

I live in a different part of town now, and while it's faster to go through Silverlake and across Beverly, I wanted to put myself in a place where I'd be most receptive to emotional sense memories, so I added twenty minutes to my drive and went down the 2, up the 5, across Los Feliz and down Western before cutting across Sunset to Van Ness. I took this route every single day, once I got my driver's license (and a license plate frame on my Prelude, the one that was just a little better than Patrick's, that said "My other car is the Enterprise" – awesome), and at one time could probably do it with my eyes closed. I told my iPod to shuffle my '80s Alternative playlist, and after an hour of Boingo, Depeche Mode, OMD, Squeeze, and The Smiths, I was, as they say, really feeling it when I pulled up to the guard gate on Melrose.

I turned down *Only a Lad* and rolled down my window. "Hi," I said, "I'm Wil Wheaton, and I'm going to Stage 24 for the *Star Trek* documentary."

The guard, who was probably in elementary school when I was piloting the Enterprise, nodded.

"May I see your ID, sir?"

Though I'm "sir" to a lot of people these days, it was bizarre to hear it in a place where I was used to

93

being "The Kid" or "The Boy." I pulled it out of my wallet and handed it to him.

"Okay, you're all set, Mr. Wheaton," he said. "Just pull up to the valet there. I'm sure you know your way around here?"

I smiled. "Yeah, I do."

He handed me back my ID and leaned down toward me.

"We're not supposed to do this, but I'm a big fan," he said, conspiratorially. With anyone who really was a big deal in Hollywood, he was probably risking his job.

"Really?" I said. "You seem a little young for TNG."

He grinned. "Not *Star Trek*, your blog."

This took me completely by surprise. I have been so busy with other writing projects that I haven't been able to give my blog the attention I want. I've frequently considered putting it on hiatus for a few months.

"That," I said, "is totally awesome. Thank you."

He smiled and then looked over his shoulder at the other guards. He turned back to me, nodded tersely, and waved me onto the lot.

I traded my car for an orange ticket with some numbers on it and headed toward stage 24. A few minutes later, I walked past the Hart building, where TNG's writers and our fearless leader Gene Roddenberry lived while I was on the series. I stopped for a minute and looked at what had been

Gene's first-story office window. I was hit by a machine-gun montage of all the times when I walked past that window and he called me in for a visit. I looked at the empty spot on the sidewalk where Gene's golf cart used to be – the same one that I frequently got into trouble for racing around the backlot. I felt the first of many tugs at my heart.

Oh boy. This is going to be one of those days, I thought, as I pulled myself back into the present and walked to stage 24 to meet the crew.

"Glad you could make it, Wil," the producer said, as my eyes adjusted from the brilliance of the day to the darkness of the empty stage.

"Me too," I said.

I looked around for a moment. Something about this place was incredibly familiar.

"Hey, you know what I just realized? I shot *Family Ties* here right before I started *Star Trek.*"

"Really?"

"Yeah, I was cast as Tina Yothers' boyfriend. I only did one episode before I booked TNG, but the word on the street at the time was that Gary David Goldberg was going to write me in as a recurring character before I went into outer space," I said. "And, uh, the future."

The stage was completely empty, except for a couple of work lights and the bleachers where audiences once sat. This stage, once filled with laughter and the energy of filming "live, before a studio audience," was now little more than an empty room. My whole life, I've been in love with the magic that goes into creating the suspended disbelief of movies and television, but it wasn't until I stood in that empty stage that I fully appreciated the effort that went into transforming 12,000 square feet of soundstage into the Keatons' lives for eight years.

"So I thought we'd head over toward stage 9," the producer said to me, "and we'll shoot our host wraps in there."

"Wait." I said. "You mean we get to walk *into* stage 9?"

"Don't get too excited," he said. "There's nothing left from *Trek* in there."

Though I knew that there was no way they'd preserve our sets for twenty years, and though I knew that someone else would eventually move into our stages, just as we'd moved into the original series' stages, I still felt a little sad.

"Nothing at all?" I said. It was a stupid question. Of course there wouldn't be anything there. But like a kid who just learned that Darth Vader was just a guy in a suit, or that KITT didn't really talk, I had to ask again, just to be sure I hadn't somehow misunderstood the cold hard reality.

"They're building sets for some reshoots on a Farrelly Brothers movie," he said, "so we'll just shoot outside." I was struck by how blasé he was, which shouldn't have surprised me. How could I expect anyone else in the world to have the same emotional attachment to those stages as I did?

"Well . . . okay," I said.

The crew got the camera and sound equipment together and loaded it on a cart that looked heavy and awkward.

"Do you know a fast – and preferably easy – way to get over there from here?" the camera man asked me.

I couldn't suppress a smile. "Yeah. I do."

We headed out of the stage and back past the Hart building.

"See that window?" I said. "That used to be Gene's office."

"Mmmm," came the reply.

Nobody is going to care about these things like you do, I thought. *Just keep it to yourself.*

I looked at the window just a little bit longer. I recalled watching Shatner's infamous "Get a Life" sketch on 3/4-inch video tape in Gene's office with some of my friends who worked there during the second season.

A few Trekkie VIPs were there on a tour, and they watched it with us. (In the pre-Internet days, it was not very easy to watch that sketch on demand – come to think of it, thanks to NBC's armada of lawyers and the DMCA, it's just as hard today). At one point in the sketch, Shatner says, "That was the evil Captain Kirk from episode 37, 'The Enemy Within' . . ." and all of the Trekkies derisively snorted, in unison, "YOU MEAN EPISODE FOUR!" I looked at my friend, who very subtly shook his head. These were Big Deal Trekkies; pointing out that they'd just brought the sketch into the real world would have created some problems.

Back in the present, I laughed out loud, and a couple of the crew looked at me. "Memories," I said.

I led them across the lot, on a route that would appear circuitous to anyone who didn't work there for the better part of four years. On the way to the stage, I passed the same familiar and significant landmarks from my youth that I wrote about in *Just A Geek*:

> That's where I met Eddie Murphy when I was sixteen . . . Hey! I crashed a golf cart there when I was fifteen . . . There's the mail room . . . There's stage six, where the bridge set started out . . . I almost got up the courage to kiss that girl at the Christmas party on that stage in . . . there's the stage where Shatner told me, "I'd never let a kid come onto *my* bridge."

The next line in *Just A Geek* is, ". . . this street feels exactly the way it did when I worked here . . . here's where my trailer used to be . . ." Though I stood in that same place, it didn't feel the same at all. Different trailers were there, filled with different actors working on different shows, but that wasn't why I just couldn't deny that twenty years had passed since I started working here. Maybe it was the knowledge that *Star Trek* is really gone for good, at least the way I knew it. Maybe it was the pain in my hip . . . or the responsibility on my shoulders. Maybe it was the fact that I have two sons who are older, and more mature, than I was when I started working on the series. Most likely, it was a combination of all those things.

I walked a bit farther, to the entrance to stages 8 and 9. In the hallway between them, where our security guard stopped tourists and Trekkies from coming onto the sets, where our bulletin board for callsheets, shooting schedules, and my brief foray into editorial cartoons used to be, there was now some sort of big, loud . . . something, with a fan and a bunch of pipes running out of it. As much as that behemoth should have prepared me, I was just gutted when I opened the stage 9 door. Instead of seeing the back of a turbolift and a corridor leading to the transporter room and engineering, I saw a bunch of sets under construction: sets that were quite clearly houses and other rooms squarely from the 21st – not the 24th – century.

Wow, I thought. *It's all . . . gone.*

I stood in that open doorway for a long time and stared, working hard to replace the reality inside the stage with the memories inside my head.

". . . ready?"

"I'm sorry, what?"

"Are you ready?" the producer asked.

"Uh, yeah." I reluctantly let the door close.

"It's too loud here to shoot, so we're set up behind the stage," he said.

I followed him down the street, past where my school room – what was effectively my entire high school experience – used to be. There was a production golf cart for *Everyone Hates Chris* there now. I lingered briefly, fighting the urge to take one more golf-cart joyride.

Moments later, we were set up in the alley behind the stage, just outside a giant open door. I looked inside. Where Sickbay used to be, there was a set that looked like a child's room. Where the holodeck once stood (and where all the shuttlecraft interiors were shot), there was a large drop cloth and a several cans of paint. Where Picard used to command the battle bridge – one of my all-time favorite sets – there was a tropical backdrop.

I sighed and blinked back some tears.

"Everything okay?" the producer asked.

"Yeah," I said. "I'm just overwhelmed by a sadness right now that I can't really explain."

"I understand," he said. "This happens whenever we work with someone from *Next Generation*. I don't know what it was about you guys, but every single one of you loved each other and remembers working on the show very fondly."

"I didn't know that," I said, around a lump in my throat. "But I'm not surprised. I . . . I really miss those guys."

For the next few hours, we filmed host wraps. I told stories about my time on *Star Trek* to anyone who would listen, and a few who wouldn't.

In front of stage 16, I recalled an encounter with Lawrence Tierney (best known as Joe in *Reservoir Dogs*), who played holodeck tough guy Cyrus Redblock.

"Hey," he said to me one afternoon between scenes, "do you play football?"

I was 15 and weighed 95 pounds . . . if I was soaking wet *and* carrying a ten-pound weight.

"Uh, no," I said.

He leaned into me, menacingly.

"Why the hell not? What are you, some kind of sissy faggot?"

I panicked, certain that he was going to beat the shit out of me because I was more comfortable throwing 3d6 than a pigskin.

"I'm not strong enough to play football!" I said.

"Well, maybe you wouldn't be so weak if you played football!" he growled.

An assistant director arrived just in time to call us to the set and save me from certain death.

"Everyone has their own story about Planet Hell," the producer said, pulling me back to 2007, "but yours is the first one that includes a fear of death unrelated to atmospheric smoke."

"Boy, we sure like to complain about that smoke. Did you know it was mineral oil-based?" I said.

"After all the cast interviews I've done over the years, I know everything in the world there is to know about that smoke," he said, dryly.

Now it was my turn to laugh.

When the day was over, we headed back to stage 24, where they were set up to interview Ron Moore.

"How's it going?" I said to him when he walked into the stage.

"It's weird," he said. "This is the first time I've been here in years."

He looked around and his voice softened. "Did you know there aren't any writers left in the Hart building? Brannon is moving out, and he was the last one. It's just a bunch of accountants right now."

"That's poetic," I said.

He looked away for a moment and furrowed his brow.

"It's just . . . I look around here and—"

"I know." I said. "I totally grok."

We talked for a few more minutes, until they were ready for his interview.

"I will kick myself later if if I don't tell you how much I continue to love *Battlestar*," I said before I left. I didn't get up the nerve to add, "and I'd really love to work on it if you have anything for me, because it's just about the best sci-fi on television, ever." Later on, I kicked myself, and delivered one more to Jenny and the wimp.

"It's always good to see you," he said.

"Thanks, man. You too."

I shook hands with everyone and said goodbye. When I got out of the stage and walked past the Hart building, I stopped and looked at Gene's old office window one last time. Though I'd said goodbye to Gene at his funeral in 1991, I said goodbye to him again – and to so many other things.

On my way back to the valet, I walked past the commissary, where I ate grilled mustard chicken with curly fries a few times a week during much of the series. I remembered a day, during the third season, when I didn't have a lot of cash on hand and no credit card, so my server got severely under-tipped. I planned to make it up to him the next day, but when I walked in, he silenced the entire commissary by running toward me from the back, screaming at me for stiffing him the day before. It was the first and last time in my life I wanted someone to be fired for the way they treated me. Strangely, I still feel bad that I unintentionally stiffed the guy. Funny how those things stay with you and come back when you least expect them to.

Just past the commissary, where there used to be a company store that sold T-shirts and satin jackets celebrating the wearer's affinity for *Cheers*, there was now a smaller company store that included a Coffee Bean. I stepped into the same room where I used to pick up really cheesy TNG T-shirts and insanely cool tiny communicator pins for my friends and family, and I bought myself an iced green tea.

I made my way back to the valet, where I traded an orange ticket with numbers on it for my car. While I waited for it to arrive, I struggled to put the nostalgia and associated sadness of the day into perspective. I didn't mourn the loss of my sets as much as I mourned the time in my life those sets represented: A time when my biggest responsibility was knowing my lines and getting to the set on time, not coming up with college tuition for the next four years. A time when KROQ played music that was relevant to me, and I knew all the DJs. A time when my biggest problem in the world was getting out of costume and makeup early enough to make it to the Forum for a Kings game. A time when my life was simpler and easier, when I had the luxury of taking for granted that I would always have everything I wanted and my opportunities were as numerous as the little mirrored stars on the black velvet starfield that hung behind Ten Forward on stage 9 . . . stars that are, most likely, cut up into hundreds of little bits to be doled out at auction for the next decade.

But, complicated as it is, I really like my life. I have a beautiful wife and two children who, though they don't carry my DNA, are clearly mine in every way that matters. I'm not going to be buying a boat any time soon, but I have been able to touch lives as a writer in ways that I never could have when I wore a spacesuit, just reading the words that other people thought I should say.

The valet brought my car around, and I gave him a couple bucks from my front pocket.

"Thank you, sir," he said.

Goddamn, it's weird to be "sir."

"No problem."

I got in my car and headed toward a red light on Van Ness, where a big decision loomed: turn left and drive back over Los Feliz, the way I always used to drive? Or make a right and head down across Beverly?

Luckily, this was an easy one. I hit my blinker and began my voyage home.

let go – a requiem for Felix the Bear

One morning a few years ago, Anne walked out into our garage to put some towels or something into the dryer. I heard the door close. A minute or so later, she called out to me, "Wil? Can you come in here? Quickly?"

There was a tiny bit of urgency in her voice, so I jumped up from the couch and ran through the kitchen, across the breezeway, and into the garage. She stood next to the dryer, a pile of wet clothes in her hands.

"Is everything okay?" I said.

"Shh!" she said, and pointed to the middle of the garage. "Listen!"

I did, and after a few moments, I heard a very soft meowing. Both of my cats were indoor cats, so I called out, "Biko? Sketch?"

I turned to Anne. "How did they get out of the house?"

She shrugged. "I don't know, but—"

A sleek black cat came walking out from beneath one of several piles of crap we have out there (putting a car into our garage is about as likely as one of us building a rocket in the backyard and colonizing the moon). He had bright yellow/green eyes, a white star on his chest, and little white "socks" on his front paws. He had no tail.

"Hey, Kitty!" Anne said. "What are you doing in my garage?"

She shoved the clothes into the dryer and crouched down on the floor. The cat began purring loudly as he walked over to her. She extended her hand and he rubbed his little face up against it.

"You are such a little Bear!" she said, as she scratched his ears.

I've seen this from her before: she was in love. She looked up at me, like a child. "Can we keep him?"

"We already have two cats, Anne," I said, "and what if someone misses him?"

"We'll wait a week and look for signs around the neighborhood. If we don't find signs, and he's still here, we'll take him to the vet and make sure he's healthy."

I've also seen this from her before: her mind was made up.

For the next week, he stayed on our patio while we looked for signs in our neighborhood. We called local shelters, pet stores, and vets, asking if anyone had reported a missing kitty. Nobody had. As far as we could tell, this kitty had just shown up out of thin air; if anyone missed him, they weren't being very vocal about it.

The first few days of that week, I tried not to get too attached to him, but whenever I walked out onto the patio, he'd talk to me a bunch. If I got close to him, he'd start to purr and rub up against my legs. He was so affectionate, it took about three days for him to win me over. I started counting down to the seventh day, when we would take him to the vet and know for sure if he could officially become a member of our family.

At the end of the week, we took him to the vet and had him checked for diseases and stuff.

"What's his name?" the receptionist asked us.

Anne and I looked at each other. Over the week, we had both loved this little guy a lot, but we'd never thought to name him.

"Oscar?" I said.

She smiled and shook her head. "No." She turned to the receptionist and said, "His name is Felix."

"Yeah!" I said. "Felix the cat!"

While we were there, we saw a picture on the wall of a cat that looked just like him, and we found out that he was a special breed called a Japanese Bobtail. Over the next few years, this would lead to our calling him "Stumpy" and referring to his activity as "just stumpin' around in the yard." His blood work came back the following day: he was free from all diseases, but his kidney levels were a little high – probably the result of him being just a little dehydrated. We know now that it was much worse, but at the time we were blissfully ignorant, and the Wheaton household grew by one.

We brought him home and introduced him to our cats. Biko was indifferent, but Sketch cranked at him right away. Ever since he was a kitten, Sketch was a daddy's – then a momma's – boy. He didn't like that there was a new kitty in our house who would be siphoning away some of his attention and affection. For the next week or so, there was a lot of peeing on the furniture, but Biko and Sketch finally accepted that this new kitty wasn't going to leave and that his arrival didn't diminish our love for them.

Felix loved us, but always on his terms. There's a saying, "Dogs have masters. Cats have staff," and so it was with Felix. He was always affectionate, but he made it clear that he wasn't our cat: we were his people. We didn't mind at all.

A few years passed, and Felix brought all kinds of joy into our lives. He had his "rotation," where he'd sleep on Ryan's bed for a week or so, then

Nolan's, then with me and Anne. Even though he was just a cat, when he put you on his rotation, you couldn't help but feel special. Chosen.

We learned quickly that Felix didn't take any shit from anyone, especially other cats. In the first year that we were his people, he went to the vet several times for shots and stitches after fights with other neighborhood cats. When he went outside, Anne and I started telling him, "Watch for cars, and don't get into any fights!" He rarely listened, but he was an incredibly tough little guy who earned his nickname "The Bear." As far as we know, he never lost a single fight.

About two years ago, we noticed that he spent a couple of days acting a little strange. He didn't want to be cuddled, and he wouldn't eat very much; he just looked like he didn't feel well. We figured it was the result of his latest fight, so Anne took him to the vet for more antibiotics. When she came home, her eyes were red and her cheeks were shiny with tears.

"What's wrong?" I said.

"The vet said that Felix doesn't feel well because he's having kidney failure. He could die within a month." She collapsed onto our bed and sobbed. I did my best to comfort her while I processed the shock of the news.

"Is there anything we can do?" I said.

"We may be able to give him special food and fluids, but—"

"Then that's what we'll do," I said. And we did. We gave him some fluids every morning, put him onto special food, and gave him a little extra love. Within a couple of days, The Bear was stumpin' around the yard, chasing birds across the grass, and curling up in our laps whenever we sat on the couch. His sleeping rotation put him into our room, and I fell asleep for many nights listening to him purr softly on my chest.

The rest of that year, he had ups and downs. One terrifying weekend Felix was rushed to the emergency vet because the gardener sprayed weed killer in our front yard – which I'd specifically told him not to do – and Felix had walked through it. During that stay at the kitty hospital, I visited him often. WWdN readers were really supportive of Anne and me, and I blogged a "note" from The Bear:

> Hi. ThiS iS FELix. My Mom AND Dad ToLD mE HoW MUCh WWDN ReADerS SupPoRteD ThEM whiLe I wAs SiCK, aND i WaNT to sAY ThANK you. ThEy LovE ME A loT AnD I KnOW THIS Was hard FoR thEM.

During that stay, we found out that his kidney disease had progressed more rapidly than we expected. He was up to about 85% failure, and he was starting to become anemic. He had lost a bunch of weight, and by now he was down to about 11 pounds. Again, we made mental preparations for the worst. Again, Felix surprised us all by bouncing right back to life.

A few weeks ago, Felix started to look and act like he felt icky, so we took him to the vet yet again. This came on the heels of Sketch's near-death experience, so my nerves were pretty frayed. "I wish I could get frequent flier miles here," I joked to the receptionist for the hundredth time. She politely pretended that I wasn't the most annoying pet owner in the world.

We ran some tests on him, and the results confirmed our worst fears: his kidneys were almost completely destroyed, and he had developed such a severe case of anemia that his body wasn't able to get any nutrition out of his food. He was, quite literally, wasting away.

It was clear that if we didn't do anything, he was going to die within a few days. We talked it over with our vet, and she told us that our options were to put Felix to sleep or to give him Epogen injections three times a week, sub-q fluids twice a day, liquid vitamins, and an aluminum hydroxyde suspension each morning. It seemed like an awful lot of stuff to do, but Anne and I talked about it, trying to figure out what was best for *Felix*. We would not prolong his life simply because we didn't want to say goodbye . . . but if we could help him feel better and have a good quality of life, then we would do whatever we could afford to do. We talked it over with his vet and decided that we'd try this out for two weeks.

"What are the odds of him bouncing back?" I asked his vet.

"If it was any other cat, I'd say very slim," she said, "but Felix is one of the toughest kitties I've ever seen. Honestly, his kidney values are so high, any other kitty would have died by now."

"Is there anything we should watch for?"

She told us what I had already heard from hundreds of WWdN readers: "Felix will let you know if he's ready to go or if he wants to stick around and try to feel better."

That was two weeks ago. For the first week, Felix perked up, but he didn't bounce back the way he always had before. He stopped being reclusive, but he wasn't as affectionate as he'd always been. I hoped against hope that he'd miraculously recover, like he always did, but it just wasn't happening. I realized that I was watching him die.

A few nights ago, I sat in my dining room and read my book. I felt something brush up against my leg. I looked down and saw Felix The Bear. He was so skinny his spine stood up on his back like Mr. Burns.

"How are you feeling, The Bear?" I said.

He let out a slow and quiet meow, and walked into the living room. He wavered when he walked, like he was unsteady, or uncomfortable, or both. When he was about fifteen feet away from me, he stopped, crouched down on the floor, and flicked his little stump.

"Felix will let you know if he's ready to go . . ."

I got up from the table and walked over to him. I felt a lump rising in my throat as I got down next to him on the floor.

"Are you done?" I said.

He flicked his stump and looked up at me. His eyes looked a little cloudy; his third eyelid was closed about a third of the way. He opened his mouth to meow at me, but no sound came out.

"Okay, Felix. Okay." I scratched his little bony head. He purred weakly and tightly shut his eyes.

I knew this moment would come, and I hoped that I'd be prepared to face it, but I wasn't. Huge sobs shook my body. Giant tears fell off my face and ran down my nose.

Ferris cautiously walked over to me from the kitchen. She stopped about three feet from me, sat down, and cocked her head to one side.

"Felix is dying, Ferris," I said. "I'm okay. I'm just sad."

She sighed and laid down on the floor with her head between her paws. She watched me while I sat there and cried.

Later that night, Anne and I had The Talk. We decided that we'd done all that we could to help him, but it just wasn't enough. He wasn't really living . . . he was just staying alive. We talked about the promise we'd made two years ago, to each other, and to Felix, that we wouldn't keep him alive just because we didn't want to say goodbye. I called the vet and had The Talk with her. We made an appointment to bring Felix in the next day.

I knew I was doing the right thing, but that didn't make it any easier. As I wrote this (and it took most of the day to write – I had to stop writing several times, just to get a grip on myself) I realized that Felix hadn't been The Bear for a long time.

As I wrote, I thought about how much I would miss him. I wrote in my blog, "I will miss seeing him stand up and stretch himself out on the trunk of Anne's car before he jumps down onto the driveway and greets me when I open my car door. I will miss him jumping up into my car and talking to me while he walks around and explores the passenger compartment. I will miss watching him sit in the grass and torment the squirrel in the tree next door. I will miss watching him stump around in the backyard. But most of all, I will miss being on his rotation. Even when he decided that four in the morning was when he needed to go outside and the best way to accomplish that was to run across our heads until one of us woke up and let him out."

Just after nine in the morning on March 30th, 2005, we said goodbye to Felix The Bear. He left peacefully and quietly, surrounded by his staff who loved him.

In the days and weeks that followed his death, I kept looking for The Bear in the usual places (not because I thought he was still alive, but out of habit) and when he wasn't there, the tears often came.

About a week after we said goodbye, his vet called.

"Mr. Wheaton?"

"That's me," I said. I don't think I will ever get used to being called Mister anything.

"Felix's ashes are here, and you can pick them up whenever you'd like."

A sob rose out of my chest and caught in my throat. At that moment, I discovered that I had created a totally illogical construct in my mind where I somehow hoped that when we took him to the vet, we would trade the sick, sad, dying Felix for the healthy, tough, stumpy little Bear we used to know.

"Mr. Wheaton? Are you there?"

Felix really is gone. He really isn't coming back, I thought.

I drew a breath to steady my voice. "Can I come and pick him up right now?"

"Sure," she said.

"Okay, I'll be right there."

Fifteen minutes later, I stood in the vet's office as one of the techs gently set a small cedar box on the counter.

"I'm so sorry, Mr. Wheaton," she said.

I tried to speak, but all I could do was nod my head as I picked it up. When I got into my car, it all came back to me: the years of giving him fluids and medicine, the ups and downs as his kidney disease progressed and he fought back, the last few weeks of watching him slowly waste away, hoping against hope for a miracle we knew wouldn't come . . . and his last night with us, which he spent mostly on Ryan's bed with his little head tucked into his right arm.

"I miss you so much, Felix," I said. My eyes filled with tears as I set the box on the passenger seat. I put on my seat belt and started my car. I pulled out of the driveway as Jeff Tweedy sang,

Far, far away
From those city lights
That might be shining on you tonight
Far, far away from you
On the dark side of the moon

I long to hold you in my arms and sway
Kiss and ride on the CTA
I need to see you tonight

And those bright lights
Oh, I know it's right
Deep in my heart
I'll know it's right

I made it about two blocks before I pulled over, put my head in my hands, and completely fell apart.

lying in odessa

The club is on the eastern edge of Hollywood, in a pretty seedy area where the cops are too busy busting crackheads to bother a poker game. To get in, you walk down an alley and knock on the door with the big red bar painted horizontally across the middle. Most of the people who play here are in the entertainment industry, so it's appropriate that it's something out of a movie.

I show the doorman a business card with the club's address written on the back, and he lets me in. I'm here for a no-limit hold-em tournament. It's the first time I've ever played in an illegal game. It's the first time I've played outside of a friendly home game. It's the first time I've ever played for money.

I buy in and get my table assignment: I'm seat six at table two. We don't start for about ten minutes, so I get a bitters and soda from the bar and try to act like I belong here.

A few weeks earlier, as we waited for the subway, my friend Shane said to me, "You play poker, right?"

"Kind of. You have a game?" I said. Since I read *Big Deal*, I've entertained notions of playing in my own Tuesday Night Game.

"You ever heard of the Odessa Room?" he said.

I shook my head. "I'm spectacularly uncool, Shane, and I live in suburbia. What's the Odessa Room?"

"It's an honest-to-goodness speakeasy in Hollywood. Twice a month they have poker tournaments."

"What are the stakes?" I said.

"You can afford it. Why don't you come with me next Wednesday?"

"Because I'm not good enough to play for serious money."

"How much money is 'serious'?" he said.

"Any," I said.

"Come on, don't be a pussy."

"I appreciate the invite, but . . ."

He took out his business card and wrote down the address.

"Think about it. If you change your mind, I'll see you there. Show this card at the door."

With a blast of warm, humid air, the Wilshire/Western train pulled into the station. Shane got into the car.

As the doors closed, he said, "Of course, if you'd rather, you can just give me 100 bucks and cut out the formality of playing."

I laughed and flipped him the bird. He gave it back as the train pulled away.

I turned his card over in my hand. His office at Walt Disney Studios on one side, the address to an illegal poker game on the other.

Sometimes, I love this town.

The Odessa's illegal nature means its unknown owners have forgone the interior decorating that would make it truly cinematic; the only thing of real value is a sound system that rivals any Sunset Strip night club. Three well-worn area rugs cover most of the cold cement floor. The indirect lighting is provided by those halogen uplights that were popular in the '80s. Twelve of them line one wall, and large cathedral-like candles sit in sconces that are nailed to the other walls. There are several enormous Samoan bouncers who watch over the entire place with bored expressions that make me a little uneasy.

Everything is portable, including the bar. When I lean against it, it rolls back a few inches.

"Watch it," the bartender says. His tone tells me that this happens all the time . . . when fuckin' new guys like me show up.

"Sorry."

I swallow hard. I think about leaving, but my money is already spent. Better not lose my nerve now. For the first time since I decided to come here, I wonder if the club's name has anything to do with the Russian mafia. Then I wonder how many of these Samoan guys have guns. *What the hell am I doing here? And where the hell is Shane?*

The game starts at 8. My watch – a gift from Sean Astin when we were promoting *Toy Soldiers* in Japan – says it's 7:55. The tables are starting to fill up, so I ask the bartender for a glass of water. I take it, tip him a dollar, and head for my table.

The blinds start out at 10-20 and double every 30 minutes.

My seat is the only empty one at table two. I put my coat over the back of my chair, stack my chips, and sit down.

Eventually, we shuffle up and deal. I soon discover that I'm surrounded by a crew of regulars who all know each other. I don't know nothin' about playin' no poker, but I know enough to understand that this puts me at a significant disadvantage.

For a game in Hollywood, there's precious little coffeehousing until Mr. Lawyer, in seat one, says to me, "Hey guy, aren't you an actor?"

I hate that question, because I always have to answer, "I used to be."

"Whaddaya mean, 'used to be'?" says the guy to my right. He's a webmaster from Long Beach who could have saved an hour on the freeway and played at the Bike, but I find out later that he comes here because he's a starfucker.

"I haven't done any acting in a long time. I'm a writer now." This answer doesn't seem to satisfy them, so I say, "I only act when something really great comes along."

That is, before my agents dumped me over the phone a year ago. Where the hell is Shane?

"What show do you write for?" says Mr. Agent's Assistant, from seat three.

"Oh, I don't work in the industry. I write books."

A knowing look passes among them. "You published?" he says.

"Yeah." I don't want to talk about myself any more. I look down at my cards and find more rags. I study them and start counting my checks.

"How'd you find out about this game?" Mr. Agent's Assistant says. Then, "Call."

The action is on me. I fold.

"I'm a friend of Shane's."

They all laugh, and I find out that Shane is the deadest of dead money. Everyone likes him, but they like his poor play even more.

"I hope you play better than he does, guy," says Mr. Lawyer.

At this point, I finally get involved in a hand, misplay it on the flop, and take a very bad beat at the hands of my new nemesis, Mr. Lawyer. I will spare you the details, other than the following exchange:

Me: "What are you doing playing that hand?"

Him: "Taking a lot of your chips, guy."

Okay, I officially hate Mr. Lawyer.

I don't play a hand for the next two levels. Mr. Lawyer busts out Mr. Magician and Mr. Webmaster, Mrs. Beautiful takes care of Mr. Agent's Assistant, and there are just five of us left at the table: Mr. Lawyer, Mrs. Funnypants, Mr. I'm A Friend of Shane's, Mrs. Beautiful, and Mr. I'm In The Music Industry.

Finally, my cards start to come, and I double through Mrs. Funnypants, a well-known comedienne. On the next hand, I find myself heads up against Mr. I'm In The Music Industry, who goes all-in. I decide that I'm on a rush and, since I've got a good chip lead on him, I stupidly call with K-9. He turns over pocket tens. I luck out and flop a king, it holds up, and I bust him out. It's the first time I've ever busted anyone out, and I feel like Howard Fucking Lederer. I sneak a look at Mr. Lawyer as I rake in the pot. He's busy shuffling his chips. Mr. I'm In The Music Industry shakes my hand as he leaves.

When the blinds are up to 150-300, Mr. Lawyer comes over the top of Mrs. Beautiful, all-in pre-flop. Mrs. Beautiful calls him before he's done pushing his chips in.

Mr. Lawyer blanches and turns over 8-9 clubs. Mrs. Beautiful flashes him a smile and turns over cowboys.

"You do *not* have two kings!" Mr. Lawyer says. I wonder if that's his "I object!" voice.

"I'm pretty sure I do," she says. *Overruled.*

Mr. Lawyer stands up. A vein throbs in his forehead. I could kiss Mrs. Beautiful right now.

He pairs his 8, but that's it. Mrs. Beautiful sends Mr. Lawyer home.

He looks at me and says, "I had to take my shot."

"Tough break," I say. "Guy."

Now it's his turn to shrug. "Next time. Next time."

I feel like a fucking rockstar for outlasting him.

Later, we take a short break before we move to the final table. The other players go to the bar, the bathroom, or just meander around the mostly empty club. I walk outside and call Shane. He picks up on the first ring.

"Hey, Wil. What's up?"

"I'm at the Odessa. Where the hell are you?"

"Have you seen the news recently? I've been babysitting executives all week," he says.

"At ten o'clock on a Wednesday?"

"Yes. It's that bad. So how are you doing?"

"Better than I thought," I say. "I made it to the final table. The regulars wish your money was here."

He laughs.

"Maybe I'll play next time." I hear a voice in the background. He puts his hand over the mouthpiece and says something back. "Look, I gotta go. Good luck."

"Thanks. Bye."

The door opens behind me, and one of the big Samoan guys raises his fist at me. I wince, until I realize that he's holding up his thumb, directing me back into the club.

"They're ready for you," he says, and walks back inside. I catch the door inches before it closes. It's incredibly heavy.

We sit down and the cards come out. On the first hand, I bust out Mr. Circus Clown. A few hands later, I bust out Mr. Drunk Guy. Goddammit, this feels great! I work hard to keep my focus and hope my hands don't tremble as I separate my chips into hundred-dollar stacks.

The blinds go up to 200-400 and that takes care of Mrs. Funnypants, who was down to the felt when we moved. I try not to get too excited, but I'm currently one off the money. That's pretty damn cool, but there's a sobering reality: if I go out next, I have as much to show for my efforts as Mr. Lawyer, and I really fucking hate that guy.

Shortly after the blinds go up to 800-1600, Mr. Director busts out Mr. I Won An Emmy, and I find myself in the money! I can't believe it!

I look at my stack: I have about 5,000, I guess, and I'm looking to make a move. Mrs. Beautiful is stacked . . . and is also the chip leader with over 13,000. Mr. Director has about 2,000 less than she does. He reaches into his jacket and takes out a Camel cigarette.

"You can't smoke in here, sir," the dealer says.

The Happiest Days of Our Lives

"What?" Mr. Director says.

"It's against the law," the dealer says.

"We're in an illegal cardroom, and you're worried about me smoking?"

"Sorry," the dealer says. "House rules."

For a moment, I think Mr. Director is going to punch him, but then he laughs.

"Fucking California," he says. We all laugh as he puts the cigarette behind his ear.

During the shuffle, Mrs. Beautiful turns to me and says, "Hey, where the hell is Shane?"

"He's . . . babysitting."

"Babysitting?! Who?"

I tell her that I'm not sure. Mr. Director offers the name of a fairly prominent studio executive, well-known for his tantrums.

"I really don't know." I'm sort of glad I don't.

For the next several hands I steal a few blinds with all-in moves, but I'm nervous every time I put all my money in; I'm really getting nothing but a bunch of small off-suit junk and the occasional medium king. The only pair I get is crabs and that also gets no callers, so I let Mr. Director and Mrs. Beautiful beat up on each other while I tread water. When the blinds go up to 1000-2000, my short stack looks a lot shorter. I have just enough to cover one or two more blind bets, and I'm hoping for a miracle.

Mrs. Beautiful is on the button, Mr. Director is the small blind, and I'm the big blind. She calls. Mr.

Director folds, and I look at my cards. There's my miracle: A-10 hearts. My heart thumps hard in my chest. This time, I hope to get called by a worse hand. I've been jamming so much, any competent player should call with just about any face card that I'm ahead of. It's clear that these guys are competent players, so I wrap my left hand around my small stacks of chips and push them toward the center of the table.

"I'm all in." I know the words come out of my mouth, but they sound distant.

Mrs. Beautiful studies her pocket cards. "Call."

Visions of doubling up and making a strong run at second, or even first, begin to dance in my head.

I stand up and turn over my cards. Mrs. Beautiful bites her lip and turns over Siegfried and Roy.

Two. Fucking. Queens.

With a gentle smile, she says, "I'm sorry."

Oh fuck me. Three outs. Come on, three outs!

The dealer knocks the table, slides the top card under the the muck, and deals out three cards. He spreads them out with a flourish, just like on TV. He flips them over and the flop is revealed: 9 hearts – 10 diamonds – 5 clubs. I make a pair, but her queens still beat me.

I'm not good enough at math to know what my odds are, but I know that I'm looking at five outs, more if a heart comes. Well, maybe I'll get lucky again.

The dealer burns and turns . . . a red deuce . . .
is it hearts or diamonds? It's a heart! The lowly two
of hearts. It's the most beautiful card I've seen
tonight. Eleven cards left now in this deck that can
keep me in this game.

The busted-out players who have stuck around
to drink surround the table. A wave of excitement
ripples through them.

"Come on, Wil!" yells Mr. Drunk Guy.

Ever since the first time I caught the World
Series of Poker years ago in the middle of the night
on ESPN, I've entertained notions of playing in the
big one. But every time I go to Vegas, I look into
those poker rooms and lose my nerve. Before
tonight, I've never had the balls to play in anything
bigger than a home game with friends. I doubt I'll
ever play in the World Series, but the way I feel right
now, I could be at the final table, staring across the
felt at Johnny Chan.

I take a deep breath and grab the back of my
chair tightly, I don't have to look at my knuckles to
know that they're white. Here comes fifth street, and
the whole thing is in slow motion: the dealer knocks
three times with one knuckle; grabs the red-backed
corner of the top card, his thumb covering the little
Bicycle cherub; and burns it away. *Was that one of
my outs? I'll never know.* His hand rests atop the
deck, and it feels like an eternity before the river is
revealed . . .

. . . and it's the queen of clubs. I go out in third
place.

Mrs. Beautiful stands up and hugs me. She smells good. Mr. Director shakes my hand, and tells me that I played well. Mr. Drunk Guy tells me how much he loves me.

I pick up my coat and go collect my money.

The girl at the bar counts out a stack of bills. Blue eyes. Pale skin. Jet black hair down her back. God*damn.*

"You've never played here before," she says.

"Nope. I didn't even know this place existed until two weeks ago."

"You should come in on a weekend night. It gets crazy in here."

"Plato's Retreat crazy?" I ask.

She gives me a blank look. I realize that she can't be older than 22.

"It was a '70s sex club in New York," I say. "Not that I went there when I was eight, or anything."

"Oh." She smiles. "Well, it gets crazy in here." She hands me my money. "You should really come back." There's a subtle flirtation. I wonder for the briefest second if it's me or the cash I am stuffing into my pocket. She takes out a shiny black business card with "Odessa" stamped on the back in red ink and writes "Jessie" on it. "This will get you in." She smiles, puts it in my hand, and holds on a little too long.

I'm enjoying this entirely too much. "I usually spend the weekends with my wife and stepkids," I say, "but I'll hold onto this."

"You do that," she says. "You want anything for the road?"

Do I.

"A bottle of water would be great," I say.

She turns around and reaches down into a box against the back of the bar. Her shirt lifts up and reveals a tattoo of ribbon, tied into a bow, just above the top of her black and red—

I really need to get out of here.

"Here you go," she says.

"Thanks. Bye." I take the bottle and walk to the door. Mr. Webmaster is waiting for me.

"Hey, you played really well," he says.

"Thanks. Too bad I got clobbered by those fucking queens."

"It happens. Can I ask you a question?"

Oh good. He wants me to introduce him to the agent I don't have.

"Sure."

"Why didn't you play on Celebrity Poker Showdown?"

"Because I'm not a celebrity," I say. "At least, not in the way it matters to Bravo."

"Aw, fuck them. You can play here whenever you want."

"Thanks, man. I appreciate that."

"Just bring Shane and his money next time."

I laugh and shake his hand.

"Will do."

I walk out the door, down the alley, and past a long line of hipsters, behind a velvet rope. They have no idea about the game. The Odessa keeps a good poker face.

Acknowledgments

I owe a tremendous debt of gratitude to everyone who reads my blog and my columns at Suicide Girls and TV Squad. Without their support and constant requests for me to write another book, you wouldn't be holding this in your hands.

I couldn't have done this without the tireless assistance, guidance, and magnificent red pen of my editor and friend, Andrew Hackard. I've worked with several different editors in my brief life as a full-time writer. Until I started working with Andrew, I didn't understand why some authors would follow certain editors to the ends of the Earth to keep working with them. I also want to thank Andrew's parents, Jim and Sandra Hackard, for creating him, making him the person he is today, and for being so supportive of our work together.

All the stories in this book were originally published online in some form or another, mostly on my blog, using the TypePad software from SixApart. Thank you to everyone there for making it so easy for me to take what's in my brain and put it on the Internets, which is a series of tubes, not a truck like some people think. Thank you to everyone at Feedburner for making it so easy for me to syndicate my content to anyone who wants to read it.

My parents, Rick and Debbie Wheaton, my brother and his wife, Jeremy and Jenn, and my sister and her husband, Amy and Andrew, have been so supportive, we're never going to get a dysfunctional reality TV show together. That's okay with me. Extra special thanks to my mom, who helped me find all the photos you see on the cover of this book.

Pink Floyd, Oingo Boingo, The Who, the soundtracks to *Kill Bill* and *Death Proof,* Verve Remixed, Wilco, and The Cure provided the always-important soundtrack to keep me motivated and focused.

Warren Ellis, John Scalzi, David Wellington, Neal Stephenson, David Sedaris, Cory Doctorow, and John Vorhaus all inspired me and made me want to be a better writer. They also write books that are exceptionally awesome, and you should go out and buy them all.

My wife, Anne, and our kids, Ryan and Nolan, always know whento encourage me to stop working, go outside, and play Frisbee for a little while. Words are not enough to express my love for them.

Aunt Val, I still miss you. I wish you could read these stories with me while we eat Sugar Pops and wait for *Fantasy Island* to start.

Christopher Suicide brought me to Suicide Girls to edit geek news. Helen Jupiter made me a columnist, and Missy Suicide gives me more creative freedom than I've ever had in a weekly gig. I love writing the Geek In Review, where some of these stories started.

Mykal Burns, Stephanie and Patrick Kirchen, Darin and Dee Miller, Ryan and Kim Kallberg, and

Dan and Sharon Goldman are awesome friends who make me feel cooler than I really am.

Lee Jones read "Lying In Odessa" and began my two-year journey through the world of poker. While I was there, Brad Willis, Paul McGuire, and the members of Team Blog at the 2006 World Series of Poker inspired, challenged, and supported me. I am a better writer for knowing and working with them.

My manager, Chris Black, and his associate Ilene Haller at Opus Entertainment do a fantastic job helping me balance acting and writing, and are always patient when I tell them I can't meet with a casting director because I'm on a writing deadline.

I would be horribly remiss if I failed to thank

_____

for all of the help he/she/they gave me. Sorry, dear readers – if you want the details, you'll have to wait for the unauthorized tell-all biography, in which I'm sure he/she/they will play a prominent role.

Finally, I always thank my ninth-grade English teacher, Mrs. Lee, who told me I was the worst writer she'd ever read and that I'd never amount to anything because I was "a stupid actor." I'll keep on doing my best to show her – and every other teacher who thinks it's awesome to insult and belittle their students – how very wrong she was.

About the Author

W il Wheaton grew up in Sunland, California in the '70s and came of age in La Crescenta, California in the '80s. As an actor, he prophetically played the writer Gordie LaChance in Rob Reiner's 1986 classic *Stand By Me* and the ultrageek Wesley Crusher on *Star Trek: The Next Generation*.

After starting his blog at *wilwheaton.net* in 2001, he discovered a passion for narrative storytelling that lead to the books *Dancing Barefoot* and *Just A Geek*, as well as regular writing jobs at Suicide Girls, TV Squad, and the Onion's AV Club. His work has also appeared in Salon and Parade Magazine.

When he isn't writing, he provides the voice of Cosmic Boy on *The Legion of Superheroes* and co-hosts *InDigital* on the Revision3 network.

This is his third book, and the second to be published by Monolith Press, which he founded in 2003. He lives in Pasadena, California.

Colophon

T his book, like all of my books, was written and designed in OpenOffice.org, a free and open source word processing suite. The first draft was assembled on a computer running Ubuntu Linux and completed on a MacBookPro. OpenOffice is cross-platform, too, which is cool. The typeface is Bookman Old Style.